# Precarious Values

# Precarious Values

## Organizations, Politics and Labour Market Policy in Ontario

### by
### Thomas R. Klassen

A joint publication of the Institute of Public Administration of Canada
and the School of Policy Studies, Queen's University

Published for the School of Policy Studies, Queen's University
by McGill-Queen's University Press
Montreal & Kingston • London • Ithaca

**Canadian Cataloguing in Publication Data**

Klassen, Thomas Richard, 1957-
   Precarious values : organizations, politics and labour market policy in Ontario

"A joint publication of the Institute of Public Administration of Canada and the
School of Policy Studies, Queen's University."
Includes bibliographical references and index.
ISBN 0-88911-885-X (bound)
ISBN 0-88911-883-3 (pbk.)

1. Manpower policy – Ontario. 2. Ontario. Ministry of Skills Development.
3. Ontario Training and Adjustment Board. I. Institute of Public Administration
of Canada. II. Queen's University (Kingston, Ont.). School of Policy Studies.
III. Title.

HD5729.O5K52 2000      331.12'042'09713      C00-930449-5

*To my mother, Paula Eva Klassen,
whose passion for learning and
inquisitive disposition are
reflected herein.*

# Contents

# Tables and Figures

## Tables

## Figures

# Foreword

*If capital is borrowable, raw materials are buyable, and technology is*
*copyable, what are you left with if you want to run a high-wage economy?*
*Only skills, there isn't anything else.*
Lester Thurow (1993, p. A21)

In a world economy increasingly defined by the global reach of production and the pervasiveness of technological change, the only real security available to both individuals and countries is to be found in high levels of education and training. Other instruments of social policy, such as health care and redistributive programs, will remain as critical to a civilized society in the future as in the past. But in this new century, nations will rise and fall in large part on the knowledge, skills and talents of the people who live within their borders.

The challenge for governments is to ensure that their citizens have full access to high-quality systems of education and training. Anything less will narrow the opportunities of future generations. Is Canada well-positioned for this world? At one level, the answer would seem to be yes. In 1996, for example, expenditures on education in Canada represented a larger proportion of GDP than in all other OECD countries (OECD 1999). Yet there still seem to be important points of weakness in our system. In comparison with many countries, our programs for training and skill development lag behind, and we have not fashioned a broad societal consensus on the way ahead in this critical sector.

Thomas Klassen's study of labour market policy in Ontario offers valuable insights into the challenges that confront us. The chapters that follow reveal a story of tension and disagreement on virtually every dimension of labour market policy and training in the industrial heartland of the country. What is the basic role of government? What is the appropriate balance between educational institutions such as universities and colleges on one hand and on-the-job training in private corporations on the other? What is the appropriate role for business, labour and equity groups in the development and implementation of programs in this sector? In many European countries, these groups play a central part in steering the process, but such initiatives have proven controversial here. Finally, that hardy perennial of Canadian politics: What is the role of the federal and provincial governments in training programs? On all of these dimensions, consensus has eluded us.

The lack of broad societal agreement on labour market policy has left new agencies developed by successive governments for the delivery of training programs highly vulnerable. In tracing the life and death of two organizations, the Ministry of Skills Development and the Ontario Training and Adjustment Board, Klassen lays bare the precariousness of policies and organizations — and ultimately of the values — that give life to training programs in Ontario.

*Precarious Values* is sobering reading. Unless Ontario and Canada more generally develop coherent training programs and organizations, we enter the future with a handicap. Klassen's book is essential reading for those who seek to maximize the opportunities for Canadians in a global century.

The School of Policy Studies is pleased to join with the Institute of Public Administration of Canada in publishing this book. The School and IPAC would also like to acknowledge with thanks the support of the Canadian Labour Force Development Board.

*Keith Banting*
*Director*
*School of Policy Studies*

# Preface

What causes government to fail at some tasks? This question is the core of this book. To understand failure, I sought to study a sphere of activity in which critical decisions seemed to be chronically erroneous. In other words, a policy field plagued by an inability of decisionmakers to arrive at satisfactory outcomes. I selected labour market adjustment policy because it is pivotal to a high standard of living and social well-being, low unemployment rates, and economic competitiveness. Training policies in North America have often been ineffective: failing to meet the needs of those to be trained and those who might hire them. Government decisions, along with the organizational structures created to implement these, have typically been disappointing and have squandered public resources.

Beginning in the mid-1980s, successive political parties in the province of Ontario — a subnational jurisdiction of ten million people — have striven to arrive at strategic and effective labour market adjustment policies. To do so, new organizations were created to design and coordinate policy. In 1985 the Ministry of Skills Development was established for this task; however, it was replaced by the Ontario Training and Adjustment Board in 1993. The board was abolished in 1996 after less than three years of existence. Both organizations spent nearly half a billion dollars a year and employed hundreds of staff. To examine the chronic failures in labour market policy required working at the intersection of the organizational dynamics, policy, and politics so as to encompass the complexity of government action: the multitude of influences, conflicts, and constraints operating to produce an outcome.

I first conceived of this study while a civil servant in the Ontario government. During my years in government I worked closely with many of the key individuals and organizations found in the pages that follow. The hands-on experience gave me a unique perspective of the policy process, while the past several years in academia provided the necessary distance and objectivity to analyze events.

My purpose in writing this book is not only to elucidate the nature of government decision making and organizational dynamics, but also to contribute to more effective public policy. Labour market policy continues to be critical for today's young people, immigrants, the unemployed, and the employers. Better-designed policies and organizations, based on a more comprehensive understanding of decision making and organizational capabilities, is what I hope this book can help bring about.

*December 1999*

# Acknowledgements

This book is the result of the work of many people, notwithstanding that my name appears on the cover. Evert Lindquist, now at the University of Victoria, has been a great supporter of the project and I am indebted to him for many insights and suggestions. At the University of Toronto, Jeffrey Reitz supplied intellectual guidance and support. Sandford Borins, Raymond Breton, Edward B. Harvey, Lorne Tepperman, and Graham White aided in the research process both by pointing to alternate explanations for events and by giving advice. David Wolfe read parts of the manuscript at several points and cheerfully gave advice.

Bernard Shapiro, at McGill University, contributed not only advice, but unbeknownst to him, a role model. Jack Richardson, from MacMaster University, brought his knowledge of organizational dynamics to bear on the research topic. Mark Waldron, at the University of Guelph, provided a treasure of documents and direct experience on training issues. My discussions with Stephen McBride, at Simon Fraser University, allowed me to broaden my perspective on labour market policy. Suzanne Leblanc, from the University of Northern British Columbia, aided in the development of the research methodology for this study. Reuben Roth, at the Ontario Institute for Studies in Education at the University of Toronto, helped me to better comprehend important aspects of the labour movement in Ontario.

Roy Bowles, Jim Conley, and Alena Heitlinger at Trent University provided ongoing encouragement for my research activities. While I was a student at Trent University the courses taught by Pradeep Bandyopadhyay, John Hillman, and Christopher Huxley sparked my academic interests that ultimately resulted in this volume. Bill Hunter, a long-time friend from

Peterborough, carefully read the manuscript and supplied a helpful economics perspective on events as well as much welcomed moral support.

Jim Turk, formerly at the Ontario Federation of Labour, aided in providing me with access to documents, as did the staff of the Federation's library. At the Archives of Ontario, Jim Suderman and his colleagues made available extensive historical papers. In this regard, two former premiers and a senior advisor allowed me to review parts of their collections at the Archives.

At Ryerson Polytechnic University, Terry Gillin provided opportunities for intellectual growth and friendship. My colleagues at the Toronto group of the Institute of Public Administration of Canada helped to broaden my understanding of how government works, while my students gave me continual inspiration as their curiosity continually reminded me of the joy inherent in learning. Massey College in the University of Toronto, with the help of John Fraser, Master of the College, furnished me with the ideal environment for research and writing.

My colleagues in the Ontario government — of which I was a member from 1986 to 1996 — contributed to the work in different ways. A particular note of thanks is due to Peter Stokes of the Ministry of Education and Brian Goodman at the Ministry of the Attorney General. The Canadian Labour Force Development Board provided financial support for the publication of the volume. A special note of gratitude is due its executive director, Lenore Burton, for her belief in the value of disseminating an analysis of events in Ontario. The Ontario government and Trent University also furnished financial support for aspects of the research.

The editor of the publication series at the Institute of Public Administration of Canada, Peter Aucoin, ensured the review of the manuscript and provided his own helpful comments. Geoff McIlroy at the Institute ably dealt with the many production and coordination aspects of the book. Keith Banting at Queen's University proved a champion of this volume while showing much patience for this novice author. At the Queen's School of Policy Studies Publications Unit, Mark Howes, Valerie Jarus, and Marilyn Banting ensured the high quality of the finished product.

The assistance of friends and family in the writing of a book — or any other major project in life — is too complex to explain. Plainly stated, without them I could not have undertaken this work. My special thanks to Janet Atkinson, Daniel Buchanan, Paul Carr, Geoff Kettel and Samia

Makhamra who not only edited, analyzed, and critiqued drafts of the text, but also furnished tolerance and support. The love of my life, Sue Han, made the final stages of the writing process pleasant and serene as only she can.

The most important patrons of the book are the 78 individuals who were interviewed for more than 180 hours. The majority of them were, or had been, premiers, Cabinet members, and senior officials in the Ontario government. Many of them acceded to requests extending far beyond being interviewed: providing documents, commenting on drafts, and generally imparting advice. Dozens of other public officials were not formally interviewed but made themselves, and their services, available for research purposes. In this regard, the staff at the Ministry of Skills Development, the Ministry of Colleges and Universities, the Ministry of Education and Training, and the Ontario Training and Adjustment Board were instrumental in helping me obtain access to documents and key participants. Without the active participation of literally hundreds of Ontario civil servants, particularly from the two organizations under study, this volume would not exist.

# Acronyms

| | |
|---|---|
| CLFDB | Canadian Labour Force Development Board (1991-1999) |
| MCU | Ministry of Colleges and Universities (to 1993) |
| MET | Ministry of Education and Training (1993-1999) |
| MoEd | Ministry of Education (to 1993) |
| MoL | Ministry of Labour |
| MSD | Ministry of Skills Development (1985-1993) |
| NDP | New Democratic Party |
| OFL | Ontario Federation of Labour |
| OPSEU | Ontario Public Service Employees Union |
| OTAB | Ontario Training and Adjustment Board (1993-1996) |

# 1

# Introduction: Precarious Values and Labour Market Adjustment Policy

*The possible forms of human organization are numerous*
*and all of them are imperfect.*
Smith and Dixon (1973, p. 221)

Explaining failure is difficult since any failure is rarely the direct result of a single cause. To account for the failure of complex organizations charged with designing and implementing public policy is particularly vexing. Forensic autopsies — and this one is no exception — shed light not only on the deceased, but also on the environment and circumstances of their birth and life. What distinguishes this autopsy is that the subjects of the procedure are organizations rather than persons: specifically, two agencies charged with developing labour market adjustment policy in Ontario.

The organizations studied in this book had short lives and this, in itself, raises the need to understand why death came so quickly. Organizations are dynamic entities with the ability to recognize threats to their existence and act accordingly to alter their objectives to ensure survival or in other ways immunize themselves from termination (deLeon 1978). Furthermore, the second organization was expressly designed to overcome the flaws of the first one. Yet it met the same fate. What happened?

The autopsy is important for three reasons. First, to advance our knowledge of organizational dynamics and innovation in general, just as a medical autopsy advances our understanding of the physiology or general principles of the operation of the human body. The very short life span of the agencies under study may also provide insights into aspects of organizational birth, life and decline that typically occur much more slowly and thus are difficult to observe. Second, the autopsy contributes knowledge about the political and policy environment in that the organizations lived and died. Third, the knowledge from the life and death of the organizations can assist in designing more robust and effective organizational arrangements and policies. Indeed, the final chapter concludes with a discussion of what a successful successor organization might look like.

The two organizations that are the focus of this book are the Ontario Ministry of Skills Development and the Ontario Training and Adjustment Board. The skills development ministry was created in 1985 by a Conservative government, reduced in size in 1989 by a Liberal administration and altogether disbanded in 1993 by a New Democratic government. The training board was first proposed by the Liberal government, instituted by the New Democrats, existing only from late 1993 to early 1996 when it was extinguished by a Conservative regime. Both organizations were charged with developing and coordinating labour market adjustment policy to ultimately reduce unemployment. To accomplish this, each organization had a staff of over 500 and spent nearly half a billion dollars annually on a variety of programs and services.

The establishment and dismantling of the organizations were costly endeavours consuming significant public resources. The tasks of the two departments were important ones, not only for their political masters, but also for society at large. Effective labour market policy — in reaction to economic, technological, and demographic change — has been a priority for Canadian governments during the past two decades (McBride 1994; Klassen 1996). If properly designed and executed, the agencies could have enhanced the responsiveness and coordination of policy contributing to the social and economic welfare of the province. Their failure resulted in ineffective and uncoordinated labour market policy with concomitant social and economic costs for individuals and society.

## ORGANIZATIONS, DEATH AND PRECARIOUS VALUES

Organizations are a visible manifestation of the central values of a society since organizations are established to achieve certain values held by particular groups (Simon, Smithburg and Thompson 1965; Zald 1990). Some values in society are precarious in that they are not widely shared or strongly held by the groups with political, social, and economic power. Organizations that sustain, or advocate for, such values in their function(s) are insecure, subject to alteration and may wither altogether as power relations shift. In other words, a socially relevant function is crucial for organizational survival and autonomy (Downs 1967).

Schools, police forces, fire departments, and hospitals are institutions integral to the functioning of modern society. The values associated with these organizations (learning, personal safety, and health) are so important to most citizens that the organizations enjoy nearly universal support. This support is tangible in that individuals and groups act in ways, such as attending schools, which perpetuate the institutions. There is little questioning as to the need, or particular design, of these organizations. At times there may be some public debate as to the number of hospitals or schools required but there is no dispute that hospitals and schools should continue to exist in their present organizational form and remain publicly funded. It is taken for granted that schools be governed by elected trustees, headed by principals, and that learning be structured into discreet units supervised by state-sanctioned teachers. Of course, initially the values associated with these organizations were much more precarious, as were the organizations themselves. Over time the values became stronger and widely shared, for example, allowing schools to acquire public funding and assume more permanent organizational structures (Tyack and Hansot 1982).

Because the Ministry of Skills Development and the Ontario Training and Adjustment Board failed to survive for very long it is logical to postulate that the values they embodied, and hence their function, were somehow precarious. Precarious values, especially as these are associated with organizations, are the conceptual starting point for the analysis and are discussed in more depth later in this chapter.

The central questions of this book can be divided, albeit with overlap, into two types: organizational and policy. The organizational questions include: What needs do new organizations have? What is the role of leadership in organizational performance? What is it about the environment that caused the organizational structures to falter? What was the congruence of the organization's function with the values of the larger society? and What can be done to make labour market policy agencies more effective and longer lived?

The policy and related questions include: What political and economic conditions, and groups, were behind the emergence of the organizations? Who decided the structure of the two agencies and what rationale was employed? What were the motivations of the key decisionmakers? Why is the labour market policy field a hazardous one for organizations? and What type of organization can effectively implement and coordinate labour market policy?

The analysis of this book targets organizations, rather than policy, although the two are intertwined. Past research has paid relatively little attention "to the processes through which particular organizational patterns have been generated ... to history, to the sequences of events and contexts through which the present arrangements have been manufactured" (Benson 1977a, p. 6). The study of organizational decline and death is a recent field, having emerged in the late 1970s as an area of study; and remains one of the least understood of organizational phenomena largely because of the paucity of empirical research (Greenhalgh 1983; Cameron *et al.* 1987; Brint and Karabel 1991; Scott 1995). The study of the two departments responds to the need to acquire "better information about the life course of institutions. Although there are many studies of the emergence of institutions, there are far fewer of the processes by which they persist over time and still fewer of their dissolution. Moreover, virtually all ... studies deal with only one of these phases, either emergence or persistence or deterioration" (Scott 1995, p. 146).

Four causes of organizational decline have been identified: (i) internal factors, (ii) external factors, (iii) the age of an organization, and (iv) the size of an organization (Hrebiniak and Joyce 1985). These act as guideposts in the next chapters by pointing to the salient variables that need to be examined. Internal factors include the manner of organizational inception, the adequacy of design, strength of leadership, and robustness of corporate culture. Leadership is particularly important because leaders must make decisions concerning "what clientele, what market to serve; ... the selection of central personnel; and the determination of the nature and timing of formalization of structure and procedures (Scott 1992, p. 66). Leaders who cannot ensure a "continued supply of resources ... and ... the satisfaction of powerful groups in [the] environment" will threaten the survival of the organization (Aldrich and Pfeffer 1976, p. 83).

External factors relate to the manner in which the organization interacts with its environment; that is, how the organization is shaped by the environment and how it in turn attempts to alter external conditions. The political and larger socio-economic milieu is critical for any department and its influence is often felt via other organizations. In this manner, other organizations are a powerful environmental influence. The ways in which organizations can interact with one another include collaboration, co-optation, cooperation, mutual adjustment, regulation, competition, and conflict. For example, competition from other agencies reflects the fact that agencies "must meet the challenge of rivals inside the machinery of government standing ready to take over their functions — and perhaps engaged in deliberate campaigns to do so" (Kaufman 1976, p. 13). The existence of rivals is a reflection of the political and policy landscape, and as will be shown in later chapters is a key factor in the demise of the two agencies.

The third cause in accounting for organizational decline is the age of an organization in that as a general rule "a higher proportion of new organizations fail" (Stinchcombe 1965, p. 148). New organizations have a higher propensity for failure, than older organizations, because they have less time to establish stable structures, processes, and relationships, both internally and externally. More recently, the liability of adolescence hypothesis has been advanced which proposes that organizational mortality is greatest *not* immediately after being established, but after a period of adolescence (Bruderl and Schussler 1990). This hypothesis assumes that organizations face only minimal risk of decline immediately after being established since they have an initial stock of resources.

The final cause of organizational decline is organizational size (Hannan and Freeman 1983). The liability of smallness hypothesis suggests that smaller organizations have higher mortality rates than larger ones. The source for the liability is that small organizations have fewer slack resources with which to react to environmental changes than do larger organizations. Smaller organizations often must compete for domain and resources with larger organizations better equipped to acquire and maintain these — staff, clients, prestige, etc. A second formulation of the relationship between size and failure postulates that mid-sized organizations are most at risk of failing (Hannan and Freeman 1977; Wholey *et al.* 1992). This liability of the middle is thought to exist because mid-sized organizations are trapped between the advantages conferred by large size (slack resources, diversification, etc.) and those of smallness (innovation, adaptation, etc.).

Precarious values are the nexus of the analysis because they link the internal and external factors discussed above. Clark (1956, 1958, 1960) first introduced the concept of precarious values to organizational analysis, conceiving of organizations as operating in a web of societal values and beliefs. He suggested that organizations that have become institutionalized are both an expression of societal values and values in themselves. In other words, values are imbedded in an organization while also existing independently of that organization. As such, the power relations that result in precarious values within the larger society become an integral component of organizations.

Schools, for example, provide a desirable good, learning, but the organization itself is highly esteemed, notwithstanding that learning could be provided in other ways. The structure of schools has become institutionalized and there is formidable support from the state, unions, parents, and other groups for schools to be structured in a particular manner.

Precarious values exist when politically, economically, and socially powerful groups disagree about the most effective means to achieve agreed-upon ends. Some values may be so precarious that only a few small organizational structures can coalesce around them. When values are somewhat less precarious, larger and more complex organizations begin to arise; however, these organizations are subject to fluctuations in power relationships among key stakeholders.

As an example, the goal of world peace and order is a shared value among many groups around the globe. However, on the question of how to achieve such a state of affairs, and what organizations are best suited to the task, there is less agreement. Hence, the United Nations and other similar organizations embody precarious values, have limited legitimacy, and face constant calls for organizational reform. A second illustration is the value shared among employers, workers' organizations, and the state that the workforce should be well trained. Yet, there is less agreement about what organizational structures are best suited to providing training, which parties should pay for the training, and what types of training should be provided. As a result, an organization charged with ensuring that workers and potential workers are well trained will operate in a highly precarious environment.

The more precarious the values associated with an organization, the less legitimacy and domain consensus the organization will enjoy for the tasks it performs. Organizational legitimacy "refers to acceptance of the formal organization by its relevant others, based on the congruence between its goals, domain and functions and the dominant values" (Hannigan and Kueneman 1977, p. 126). Like other resources, legitimacy "can be viewed as a resource which a given ... organization attempts to obtain and which, occasionally, competing organizations may attempt to deny" (Dowling and Pfeffer 1975, p. 125).

Domain consensus is the degree of agreement among key stakeholders of an organization's proper territory and scope of activities, including clients, services, etc. (Levine and White 1961). "The higher the consensus of an organization's domain, the easier it will be for its members to conduct routine" business (Scott 1992, p. 193). Legitimacy and domain consensus are arduous to obtain for organizations facing multiple constituencies with often conflicting values and expectations. In summary, precarious values will cause an organization to have marginal status, low legitimacy and lack of domain consensus, making organizational survival uncertain (Whetten 1981, 1987; Chaison, Bigelow and Ottensmeyer 1993).

The focus on precarious values places this book in the tradition of institutional analysis which draws attention to the external environment of organizations. This environment is not only the technical one (the type of service or product produced, efficiency of production, or type of clients, etc), but also the institutional environment: the values, norms, rules, and requirements to which organizations must conform if they are to gain legitimacy and survive.

Traditional institutional analysis (Selznick 1949; Gouldner 1954; Clark 1958) has focused on the tasks that an organization is created to accomplish, and how those are altered by changes in societal attitudes and trends.

Studies typically have examined how organizations were constructed and became institutionalized. The more recent "new" institutionalism is concerned with the functioning, rather than genesis, of organizations (Brint and Karabul 1991). It conceives of organizations as bound closely to specific social rules, routines, norms, and rituals with little ability to change (DiMaggio and Powell 1991).

Churches and cultural and educational organizations have been of interest to both old and new institutionalists because they have strong institutional environments. In other words, the efficiency and effectiveness of these organizations are difficult to measure, in part because they seek to alter values and beliefs rather than just to produce a standardized product. In environments permeated by precarious values, organizations are judged, primarily, by the degree to which they conform to the values, rules, and requirements of the individuals and groups in power. In such environments organizations are largely "rewarded for utilizing correct structures and processes, not for the quantity and quality of their outputs" (Scott 1992, p. 132).

The outputs of the training ministry and board were not amenable to a simple economic cost-benefit calculus. Both organizations were charged, in part, with creating a "training culture" in the province, by designing and implementing fundamental, yet ill-defined, changes in labour market policy and in the behaviour of business, labour, training institutions, and other government departments. The very shifts in the terminology in this policy field provide an initial clue to the existence of precarious values. The terms to describe the functions of the two agencies have shifted over the past decade and a half from manpower training to skills development or training, and most recently to active labour market or labour force development policy.

Past studies of organizations almost invariably examined successful efforts of adaptation to the environment. For example, Clark (1958) in his study of adult education schools found that institutional insecurity was minimized when the organizations aligned their procedures with those of other schools. That is, they adopted the norms and behaviours (around curriculum, role of teacher, etc.) of primary and secondary schools, no matter that these were often inappropriate for adults. Selznick (1949) studied a similar situation showing how co-optation by powerful groups allowed an innovative government environmental management agency to survive and become institutionalized. The agency gained support from key stakeholders and prospered but at the cost of subverting some of its public policy objectives to private interests.

Zald and Denton found that the Young Men's Christian Association was able to persist in a society that was becoming less and less religious by transforming its original religious values and goals to "become a general leisure-time and character-building organization" (1963, p. 215). Brint and Karabel (1989, pp. 214-20) illustrate how community colleges in the United States were forced into a particular niche because of the existence of other postsecondary institutions. Although shaped and constrained by other educational institutions, business interests and governments, colleges were able to secure sufficient autonomy to pursue their own interests and become institutionalized.

Among the most precarious organizations are sects and other (small) religious movements. Often such organizations seek to bring about changes in society; however, they find that doing so is "a precarious task for a church which may easily fail" to accomplish it (Thung 1976, p. 322). Consequently, churches reduce the likelihood of organizational failure by minimizing the claims they make to being able to ameliorating social problems and by paying special attention to effective leadership as a means to increasing their legitimacy. The inability to align organizational objectives with changing societal values can lead to the extinction of religious, and other, organizations. For example, the decline of Catholic convents and female orders in North America has been caused by shifting societal values: the feminist movement, the expansion of employment opportunities for women, and changing religious convictions (Ebaugh 1993, p. 162-71).

The two agencies under study — the skills development ministry and the training board — faced environments not dissimilar to those faced by churches and the other organizations discussed above. As reviewed in the second part of this chapter and in later chapters, the organizations operated in an environment permeated by fundamental disagreements about the appropriate role of the state; federal-provincial, and intragovernmental conflicts; historical animosity between key stakeholders (business and labour); and a general inability to measure the benefits of training services. Furthermore, in the last two decades, as governments have generally abandoned Keynesian macroeconomic policies to stimulate employment, they have begun to rely on new institutions to formulate and execute training policies. This heightened the attention accorded training and further caused policies to veer sharply depending on the political parties in power and the relative strength of groups outside the state such as business and labour. Given these conditions, it seems logical to place precarious values at the centre of the conceptual framework for the forensic autopsy of the two organizations.

## CONDUCTING AN AUTOPSY

The primary source of data on the organizational, policy, and political dynamics examined in the next chapters derives from 78 in-depth interviews with key participants, a review of documents, and participant observation. Often considered of secondary importance, a full account of the methodology should be of concern to all readers. Like medical autopsies, a clear delineation of techniques and tools used, and the rationale for selecting these rather than others, strengthens the reader's confidence in the conclusions.

The organizational corpse is less readily identifiable than that for a medical autopsy. Documents and records — Cabinet reports, letters, speeches, budgets, and so forth — remain for analysis and these are helpful in reconstructing the course of events, but less useful for explaining why events developed as they did. Interviews, with premiers, Cabinet members, senior bureaucrats and leaders of the training ministry and board, along with leaders of the key stakeholders of the two agencies, provide insight into the motivations, constraints and objectives of decisionmakers.

A shortcoming of many studies of organizational and policy failures is that the researcher appears only after the death has occurred. Even if social scientists could predict failure and the exact timing of the events, the actors in declining organizations are more concerned with organizational, and career, survival than with academic research. Organizational growth and policy success has been studied more extensively because leaders of such organizations are more willing and interested in sharing their triumphs (Greenhalgh 1983). Furthermore, researchers often prefer "to focus on beginnings not endings" because these are less complex and easier to chart

(Frantz 1992, p. 175). Finally, studies of demise often aim to highlight the resilience of organizations and their ability to survive even if their *raison d'être* has been outmoded. For example, Katzenbach showed that even though the horse calvary was obsolete by the late 1800s, the US Calvary "maintained a capacity for survival that borders on the miraculous" enduring through the Second World War (1958, p. 212). This study, on the other hand, examines the opposite: rapid, although not uncomplicated, decline.

The research for this book began while the skills development ministry still existed and before the training and adjustment board was created. The author does not claim supernatural powers, merely the fortuitous confluence in his research interests and the whereabouts. From 1986 to 1996 the writer was a senior policy advisor within the Ontario public service, working in the labour market policy field, but not within the two agencies under study. This insider status allowed him access to documents that are unavailable to outsiders as well as a rich knowledge of the culture and personalities critical in the history of the two departments. Consequently, there is significant analysis of intra-organizational dynamics and of the manner in which key individuals shaped events within the broader, social, economic, and political pressures and forces. A further discussion of the research methods, the positions of those interviewed, and the influence of the author's insider status are contained in Appendix B.

The structure of this book is as follows. The remainder of this chapter examines the key features of the policy field within which the Ministry of Skills Development and the Ontario Training and Adjustment Board operated. Chapter two analyzes how the skills development ministry emerged in Ontario in 1985 and its early successes. The third chapter examines the organization's difficult middle years and its decline in the late 1980s. The rise of the training board from the ministry's ashes is traced in chapter four, while chapter five chronicles the short, albeit not uneventful, life of the training board to its death in early 1996. Conclusions and lessons — for organizational design and policy — from the two organizational failures are presented in the final chapter. Appendix A provides the *dramatis personae* and a chronology of events which may be useful in orienting the reader to the territory and events under study. Appendix B outlines the research methods utilized to study the events.

## ACTIVE LABOUR MARKET POLICY AND TRAINING

This section briefly sketches the nature of active labour market policy, especially training, in Canada highlighting the rationale for, and nature of, the involvement of the state in this field in the past several decades. Active labour market policy can have five components: (i) information provision and counselling; (ii) subsidized or created employment; (iii) training; (iv) tax policies; and (v) subsidies for worker relocation. In Canada, there are no significant tax policies aimed at mobilizing the labour supply or subsidies for workers wishing to relocate geographically, hence only the first three components can generally be identified in the Canadian context.

Active labour market policy attempts to facilitate the movement of persons into the labour force and jobs; while passive labour market measures, on the other hand, simply provide income support to the unemployed, such as unemployment insurance and social assistance (welfare) benefits. An effective, active labour market policy improves the access of individuals to jobs and ensures the efficient functioning of the labour market (OECD 1993). The more effective the active labour market policy of a jurisdiction, the lower should be its unemployment rate, especially the structural component, and the more productive its workforce.

The provision of information and counselling by the state is the most basic and least costly component of active policy. Timely information about labour market conditions and the availability of jobs allows workers to make rational choices and can foster the mobility of labour. Even in countries favouring a strong *laissez faire* posture to state involvement in the labour market, supplying information is seen as indispensable (Lester 1966). The dissemination of information and provision of counselling is typically carried out by local centres either directly by state officials — usually in tandem with the processing of applications for (un)employment insurance or social assistance — or contracted to third-party agencies. Of course, the state is not the only actor providing labour market information and counselling. Classified advertisements in newspapers and other forums, job-search agencies, trade and professional publications, and educational institutions perform this function as well, although typically only for specific groups such as in-school youth, members of a profession or trade, and so forth.

The second component of active labour market policy is the creation by the state of new employment in the public sector or the subsidization of private-sector wages. These are Keynesian strategies to expand the total employment in the economy typically utilized as short-term measures in response to recessions and high unemployment rates. However, these types of policies have become less common in the past quarter century as state expenditures have been constrained and the dominant economic and political ideology focused on reducing inflation. Consequently, Western nations have largely abandoned the Keynesian prescription of generating sufficient demand, through New Deal type job-creation policies, to ensure high levels of employment.

Training is the final component of active labour market policy having as its objective an increase in the knowledge and skills levels of the labour force. "Training not only provides a means of filling vacant jobs that require particular skills, but also may enhance the capacity for workers to be innovative and responsive to changing technology and market demands. This is the role of training in promoting economic growth. It is not possible to have an advanced technical industrial society with an untrained and uneducated workforce" (Meltz 1990, p. 284).

Effective training policy is beneficial to employers who have access to a productive highly trained workforce; while for workers, training reduces the risk of unemployment and increases wages. Training can also promote greater equity in the labour market by upgrading the skills of groups (such as women, disabled, and the visible minorities) that have been excluded from some types of jobs. Training is more costly and interventionist than the provision of labour market information, but usually less so than creating or subsidizing employment. As Keynesian policies, job creation and wage subsidies, have fallen out of favour, training has become more prominent in government policies.

Conceptually, education and training have few differences although training is generally viewed as being more job-focused and prepares individuals directly for a specific job. Both education and training are investments in human capital in that "both denote the acquisition of skills that enable people to enhance their stream of future earnings by acquiring the ability to perform a wider range of occupations, including more highly paid occupations" (ibid.). Education, however, is a far less precarious value in Canada than training because education is widely agreed to be a social good, while training is less so. This is illustrated by the near universal support for public education along with the monopoly of state-certified schools and teachers in providing education. A basic level of education is valued because it is a fundamental prerequisite for citizens to participate in society; while more advanced education confers societal benefits (in addition to individual ones) which could not be obtained without state support. The provision of training, on the other hand, is perceived to be primarily the responsibility of employers, employee organizations, and individuals rather than the state.

Unlike primary, secondary, and postsecondary education, there is no state-sanctioned set of institutions charged with the provision of training. Training services are funded from a variety of sources: employers, labour and professional groups, individuals, and the state. The delivery of training is accomplished through an array of organizations including private vocational schools, community agencies, employers, labour and professional organizations, and other private vendors in addition to community or technical colleges, universities, and school boards. Furthermore, unlike education, training can take place either in an institutional environment or on the job. Finally, to be effective the mix of training provided needs to be responsive to the demands of the labour market to avoid training people for yesterday's jobs.

A significant degree of training occurs in Canadian workplaces with surveys finding that between 11 and 36 percent of Canadian workers receive some training annually from their employers (Hum and Simpson 1996, p. 39, Table 4.1). Approximately 50 percent of Canadian employers, typically the larger ones, provide training to some of their workers during a given year (Ekos Research Associates 1996, p. 7, Table 2.1). In addition, many Canadians obtain training through other means: from union and other employee associations or through their own purchase of training services. The content of training varies significantly. At one end of the spectrum lies training required for many highly skilled manufacturing occupations as well as construction, mechanical, and repair trades. Often such skills must be obtained via apprenticeship, which involves several years of in-school and on-the-job training within a highly prescribed and rigorous format. At the other end of the spectrum is training for generic skills such as communication and the use of basic computer technology.

Individuals who are not employed, and who do not have extensive private resources, cannot benefit from employer-based training or purchase their own training. It is for this group — workers who have been laid off or are otherwise unemployed, youth, immigrants, and social assistance recipients — that training is provided by the state. With training, this group, ideally, is able to more quickly obtain and retain employment. The rapidity of technological change has placed added emphasis on training since often unemployed workers require some upgrading of skills to become employed.

Because information provision and counselling is accepted as a legitimate role of the state and subsidized employment measures are typically temporary (and in any case less common than in the past), policymakers have turned their attention to training. Indeed, during the 1980s and 1990s, "labour market policy, particularly training and upgrading the skills of the labour force, has assumed greater conceptual importance as a potential solution to economic difficulties" (McBride 1994, p. 268). Total federal and provincial expenditures in Canada on active labour market adjustment are difficult to estimate, but are likely in the neighbourhood of about five billion dollars per year. The number of persons annually provided with federal training and related programs ranged from 425,000 to over 600,000 during the late 1980s and early 1990s (Haddow 1995a, p. 355, Table 1).

Notwithstanding the growing prominence of training, the involvement of the Canadian state in funding, supervising, and coordinating training has remained precarious. The pluralism associated with this field, which grants groups outside the state a large stake in funding and delivery, is a contributing factor in making the state's role less legitimate than it has in education or health policy. Further limiting the state's legitimacy is the difficulty in tailoring training to meet the specific and changing labour market demands. The mix of skills demanded by the marketplace is difficult to predict, the possibility of error looms large, and the consequences of errors entail a misallocation of state resources.

## THE CANADIAN CONTEXT

In addition to the precarious nature of labour market adjustment and training policy discussed above, state policies in Canada related to training
have suffered from five specific shortcomings: (i) an historical dependence
on immigration; (ii) insufficient spending on active measures; (iii) inter-
and intragovernmental conflict; (iv) reliance on institutional training; and
(v) lack of organization of business and labour interests. After a review of
these immediately below, federal initiatives to address them in the past
two decades are examined. The federal activities, driven by political and
economic shifts, form one backdrop for the events that transpired in Ontario.

Historically, Canadian immigration policy has been utilized to address
skills shortages and inadequacies in the labour force (Beaujot 1991;
Veugelers and Klassen 1994). However, the introduction of a non-racist
immigration policy during the 1960s, and the changing preferences of highly
trained immigrants, has meant that immigration has become a less important tool in increasing labour market skill levels. The past reliance on immigration, however, created a legacy of insufficient investment in training
by both the state and the private sector. The ability to import skilled workers has meant that training has not been embedded as a strong cultural
value in Canadian society. For example, in Canada apprentices comprise
only 1.1 percent of total employment, in comparison to 7.4 percent in
Austria and 7.1 percent in Germany (Wilson 1993*a*, p. 33).

Canada "has always relied more heavily on the coercive force of unemployment as an 'adjustment' mechanism than have European countries"
(Giles 1989, p. 241). Notwithstanding that Canadian unemployment rates
have historically been higher than those in other OECD countries, expenditures on active labour market measures have been small vis-à-vis passive measures (Schmid 1994, p. 30, Figure 1.8; Campbell 1992, p. 27,
Table 2.1). In 1990, just over 20 percent of total Canadian labour market
expenditures were on active programs; a figure exceeded by 18 of the 21
OECD countries (OECD 1993, p. 42, Chart 2.2). In comparison, Sweden,
Germany, Norway, and other countries spent over 40 percent on active
measures and typically have low unemployment rates and internationally
competitive workforces (Schmid 1994, pp. 29-38).

Jurisdiction for active labour market policy has historically been divided between the federal government and the provinces. The close connection between training and the labour market has allowed training to be interpreted as a joint federal-provincial jurisdiction since the federal government has constitutional responsibility for macroeconomic policy. The provision of information, counselling, subsidized employment, and training for those in receipt of federal income support, primarily (un)employment insurance, as well as for the disabled and recent immigrants has been the responsibility of the federal government. Provinces have provided some of the same services primarily for social assistance recipients and the long-term unemployed who are not eligible for (un)employment insurance. Both levels of government have also tended to provide services for youth and other disadvantaged groups.

The federal-provincial dynamics of training policy have resulted in four types of intergovernmental conflict. First, although the federal government has historically funded the training of those on federal income support, much of their training occurred in the educational institutions (usually community or technical colleges) administered by the provinces. As such, the federal policy shifts have had a direct impact on the viability of the provincial training institutions. Second, some provinces have had concerns that the federal government underspent on training activities within their jurisdiction. Third, as eligibility for federal income assistance and training programs was restricted in the 1980s and early 1990s, provinces were forced to provide services to those excluded from federal programs.

Finally, in response to the federal unilateralism evident in this policy field, some provinces, notably Quebec and Alberta, have sought greater control of training expenditures while the federal government historically has been unwilling to grant such autonomy fearing a balkanization of labour market policy. As discussed later in this chapter, in 1996 the federal government offered to transfer to the provinces the bulk of its expenditures on active employment measures. Under the federal-provincial agreements that ensued, the federal government began to withdraw from the purchase of training and related services, and to transfer the employees in its network of local employment centres to the provinces (Klassen 1999a, b).

Not only is there federal and provincial conflict over training, but there is conflict between different provincial departments. Provincial education departments have tended to promote policies that safeguard funds for the community colleges, while other departments seek to expand funding for on-the-job training. As a result, there is "no single coherent framework for shaping training objectives in response to the needs of both our economy and our workers. This ... problem largely derives from the almost total absence of coordination in policy formulation and implementation between different levels and branches of government" (Wolfe and Yalnizyan 1989, p. iii).

The fourth shortcoming of Canadian training policy — an overemphasis on institutional training — comes about for three reasons: the nature of capitalism, the efforts of provinces to channel training funds to the colleges, and the resistance of some unions to on-the-job training. In a free market economy there is little incentive for firms to pay for on-the-job training since they cannot be sure of retaining the skilled workers. "Thus, on-the-job training is little used not because it is technically inefficient (it apparently is very efficient technically) but because it does not pay" (O'Connor 1973, p. 112).

Training is delivered by a variety of organizations, including government agencies, secondary schools, colleges, unions, private vocational schools, community organizations, and employers (Economic Council of Canada 1992). Nevertheless, supported by provincial government policies the colleges dominate in providing training. In contrast, in Germany, between two-thirds and three-quarters of all workers receive an average of two to three years of vocational training of which three or four days are on the job and only one or two days are in the classroom (Wever 1995, p. 101). Thus, the reliance on institutional training in Canada "is radically at variance with the pattern in most other countries" (Haddow 1995, p. 340). Finally, as discussed in later chapters, public-sector unions (representing teachers and instructors in public colleges and schools) are generally opposed to on-the-job training since it threatens the employment of their members.

The final shortcoming of Canadian training policy is that "the structure of Canadian labour and business organization is highly decentralized and fragmented" (Riddell 1986, p. 44). There are hundreds of business associations which are not organized under a single umbrella and pursue different objectives. For example, in 1989 a federal advisory council on labour market adjustment recommended that as "an incentive to stimulate private sector training ... the government establish a tax liability" on those firms that fail to invest sufficiently in training (Advisory Council on Adjustment 1989, p. xviii). Some business groups and larger corporations supported the recommendation, yet it was rejected by most others. A similar decentralization of power is found within organized labour. Decision-making power rests with individual unions and no single organization represents all unionized workers, and in any case most workers are not members of unions.

In summary, active labour market policy, especially the training component, is permeated by precarious values. There is a lack of consensus between business and labour, between the federal and provincial governments, and between industrial (on-the-job) and institutional trainers. This has left policies susceptible to shifts in power relationships among and within these groups, and to shifts in economic conditions.

## FEDERAL POLICY SHIFTS

During the 1960s the federal government's role in active labour market policy was two-fold: first, to contribute 75 percent of the capital costs for provincial training and vocational institutes and second, to subsidize the costs of the unemployed attending the institutes. Historically, the bulk of federal expenditures on training have been allocated for the purchase of training from provincial educational institutions, largely the community or technical colleges. However, with the creation of the federal Department of Manpower and Immigration and the enactment of the *Adult Occupational Training Act* in 1966, the federal government began moving from a passive to a more active role in the flow of training funds to the provinces. Rather than participating in cost-shared programs which responded to provincial desires to expand the colleges, the federal government began to purchase specific types of training from colleges (Dymond 1973, pp. 100-08). The change in policy gave the federal government some control over its expenditures and allowed, in theory, at least, better targeting of its funds.

During the 1970s the federal government emphasized Keynesian job-creation programs in response to increasing unemployment rates. However, by the 1980s policymakers became increasingly concerned about training for a variety of reasons: globalization of the economy, rapid technological change, and pressures to better target spending due to decreases in government budgets.

In the early 1980s a general consensus among key stakeholders emerged that "the training system at the present time is not fully capable of meeting the demands that will be placed upon it during the 1980s" (Canada. EIC 1981, p. 205). This shift occurred after governments began "to downgrade job creation and to stress training" (McBride 1992, p. 146). As a result there was agreement among many Western governments that if "the quantity and quality of ... training and retraining is inadequate, there is a case for [state] intervention to correct this" (OECD 1984, p. 8). The liberalization of trading arrangements such as the Free Trade Agreement with the United States in 1988 (and later the North American Free Trade Agreement) further heightened the role of training in Canada as a response to increased levels of economic competitiveness.

With the 1982 *National Training Act*, the federal government began a slow march toward trying to achieve a more active labour market policy. A major objective of the 1982 policy was to encourage industrial (on-the-job) rather than on institutional (classroom) training because federal officials saw industrial training as more effective, and less costly, in training workers. The Act also sought to encourage more private-sector involvement in training and to augment training for more advanced skills.

The 1982 reforms were only marginally successful in changing the status quo — partly because of provincial resistance — causing the new federal Progressive Conservative government in 1985 to introduce "a less Keynesian, more interventionist supply side management approach to human resource development" (Prince and Rice 1989, p. 273). The Canadian Jobs Strategy reinforced the earlier policy by attempting to direct more funding to third parties (community-based groups and private trainers) rather than to the provincial institutions. Furthermore, it tried to increase the role of business in directing federal training expenditures. Private-sector committees were established in some provinces to provide advice on local training needs and were given some funds with which to purchase training. Overall, the policy was "more selective in client programming, more decentralized in decision making [and] more privatized in delivery" than previous initiatives in this area (ibid.).

Although the 1985 policy shift met with some success, federal policymakers, along with some unions and employer groups, cast wistful glances toward the European models of active labour market adjustment policy that relied on the corporatist model of decision making. Corporatism refers to institutionalized involvement and cooperation of a small number of societal interest groups in the making and sustaining of state policies (Schmitter 1974). In Germany, Austria, Sweden, and some other countries corporatism allowed business and labour to be partners with the state in designing labour market policies. Beginning with the 1989 Labour Force Development Strategy the federal government redirected further funds from passive to active measures and made a commitment to involve business and labour in decision making around training.

A major organizational innovation occurred in early 1991 with the establishment of a national training board — the Canadian Labour Force Development Board (CLFDB) — modelled after the corporatist arrangements in Europe. The board was composed of 22 representatives: eight from each of business and labour and four from social action groups (women, the disabled, visible minorities, and Natives) and two representatives from training providers. The members of the board were nominated by the constituencies: almost 90 national organizations. Decision making was by consensus and the board was co-chaired by business and labour.

The board's function was to advise the federal government on training expenditures with the expectation that over time it would take on a larger role in developing policy. The agency was established quickly and without a legislative mandate with the attitude, as one participant noted, "of let's see if this thing will work." The CLFDB operated with an annual budget of between two and three million dollars and just over a dozen staff.

In late 1991 the CLFDB, along with the federal government, formally proposed that the provinces create provincial training boards and that local training boards be established jointly by the federal and provincial governments to complement the national and provincial bodies. Many provinces — British Columbia, Saskatchewan, Ontario, New Brunswick, Nova Scotia, and Newfoundland and Labrador — did establish provincial boards. The boards generally mirrored the CLFDB composition, although some provinces added one or two seats for specific groups. In Quebec a somewhat different body, the Société Québécoise de développement de la main d'oeuvre, was established in 1993 to direct provincial training programs.

The Ontario and Quebec agencies were by far the largest and the only ones with decision-making, rather than merely advisory, powers.

The establishment of the labour force boards was a unique and innovative accomplishment in Canadian labour market policy. The boards showed that business, labour, and the state could find sufficient common ground to at least sit at the same table to address the economic imperatives bearing on all three. Corporatist models have been effective in coordinating and centralizing policy in European nations and there was no *a priori* reason why they could not begin "overcoming the historic barriers to corporatism in Canada" (Mahon 1990, p. 89). Indeed, because the degree of corporatism in Canada is low, in comparison to other developed countries (Dell'Aringa and Lodovici 1992, pp. 32-33, Table 2), it seemed logical that a higher level of corporatism would be attainable, even if that might be considerably less than in European countries.

However, the creation of the boards did not necessarily mean that agreement on policy had been reached; the parties merely agreed to sit at the same table. The existence of boards was proof only that corporatist mechanisms could be crafted, not that they could operate effectively. Nor did the joint boards imply that business and labour were willing to shoulder a greater share of the cost of training, as is the case in the European corporatist model. Thus, as the boards were being designed in the early 1990s it was unknown the extent to which the fragmentation within business, labour, and the state concerning training and the antagonistic nature of business-labour relations could be overcome by new organizational arrangements. In other words, unanswered was whether the corporatist boards could make training more secure and less precarious.

As the 1990s progressed it became apparent that most boards were proving to be unsuccessful and indeed the majority have now been terminated (a history of each board is found in Sharpe and Haddow 1997). The history of the CLFDB is an example of the fate met by several other boards. Its powers were first reduced when the Liberals assumed power in Ottawa in 1993; and in 1999, after eight years of operation, the decision was made to disband the board altogether. The Quebec board has been the most successful in part because of unique social and historical conditions in the province that foster corporatistism (Haddow 1998). The Ontario board, whose fate is analyzed in chapters five and six, was the most ambitious corporatist model ever instituted in Canada. The concluding chapter examines how the experience in Ontario, and by extension other jurisdictions, can be beneficial in guiding future developments in labour market policy.

The failure of the corporatist boards along with larger political events provoked the most recent restructuring in labour market adjustment policy: the implementation of federal-provincial labour market agreements. These agreements transfer the bulk of previously federal policy and program responsibility to the provinces. Quebec provided the spark for this transfer since the province had for decades argued that social and economic developments are closely linked and that adequate integration and coordination is impossible if the federal government controls labour market policy (Canada. House of Commons 1995, pp. 286-92). This demand was acceded to in the 1992 Charlottetown Accord, which offered to transfer all training activities and labour market development activities, except unemployment insurance to interested provinces. Matters remained unresolved until the Quebec referendum in late 1995 when Prime Minister Jean Chrétien committed to withdraw from "training" (the scope of which was undefined).

On 30 May 1996, the federal government made public its offer: the transfer to the provinces of $1.5 billion of expenditures on active employment measures as "an important step towards a more flexible federalism" (Canada. HRDC 1996). The labour market development agreements that were signed with many provinces following the offer allow for the transfer of most of the funding allocated for active labour market measures to the provinces, including wage subsidies to employers, earnings and income supplements to individuals on (un)employment insurance, and loans and grants to individuals for the purchase of training. The agreements also allow provinces to assume responsibility for counselling and placement services for (un)employment insurance clients (Klassen 1999a, b). In Ontario alone, more than 1,000 federal staff and nearly $0.5 billion will be conveyed to the province once an agreement is reached. The labour market agreements are a significant shift in the intergovernmental regime in the training field that highlights the *leitmotif* of this book: How can provinces design effective policies and organizations in labour market adjustment?

In conclusion, the abandonment in the 1970s of Keynesian prescription by Western governments and their replacement by monetarist and post-

Keynesian solutions increased the emphasis on training. By removing one policy lever — creating state-subsidized employment — greater stress was placed on the remaining tool: training. Consequently, policymakers were faced with designing organizational structures that would ensure effective training policies. The corporatist training boards represented one solution to this challenge, while the devolution to the provinces is the latest answer to making training more effective. The search for solutions illustrates how historical conditions in Canada (previous reliance on immigration), state dynamics (jurisdictional conflicts), organizational imperatives (the power of the colleges), and the nature of capitalism (limited role for the state, fragmentation within business and labour, and labour-business conflict) continue to make training policy precarious. The next chapter begins by tracing the developments in this field in Ontario and the manner in which they gave rise to the Ministry of Skills Development in the mid-1980s.

# 2

# The Rise of the Ministry of Skills
# Development: Turmoil and Opportunity

*Magnificently unprepared*
*For the long littleness of life.*
Frances Cornford (1886-1960)

The beginnings of active labour market policy in Ontario can be traced to
the *Ontario Industrial Education Act* of 1911. The Act recognized that, in
a rapidly industrializing and urbanizing environment, schools were required
to provide vocational and technical education in addition to a general education. Consequently, the Department of Education established numerous
technical secondary schools throughout the province.

The creation of technical schools and the provision of vocational education by the education department in the 1910s and 1920s did not eliminate
shortages of skilled employees in all occupations. The 1928 *Ontario
Apprenticeship Act* laid the foundation for the creation of a largely "on-
the-job," provincially supported, skills training system. When the Act was
passed the government faced the decision as to whether apprenticeship
should be administered by the education department or the Department of
Labour. The business community successfully lobbied to make certain that
the labour department would manage apprenticeship. Business feared that

if located in the education department, "apprenticeship might be subverted to institutional priorities of that department" becoming distant and unresponsive to labour market conditions (Dupré *et al.* 1973, p. 61). Thus, beginning in 1928 industrial training, primarily apprenticeship, was nurtured and administered by the Department of Labour.

Beginning in the late 1940s the Department of Education created additional postsecondary educational institutions, the institutes of technology, for the purpose of vocational education and training. These new institutions included the Ryerson Institute of Technology, now Ryerson Polytechnic University and the Lakehead Technical Institute, now Lakehead University among others.


## PRE-HISTORY


By the 1960s dual systems of skills training had emerged in the province: industrial (on-the-job) and institutional (classroom). These systems embodied different philosophies and became lodged in different organizations. The labour department developed vocational training within industry, administered directly by provincial officials, while the education department funded institutional training, administered indirectly through the educational institutions. The educationalists (or institutionalists) viewed industrial training as narrow, preparing workers for a specific job without the skills and knowledge required to adapt to workplace and labour market changes. Industrial trainers and labour market economists, on the other hand, viewed institutional training as unresponsive to, and divorced from, the demands of employers.

The labour department began to expand its activities in industrial training in the mid-1960s with the replacement of the *Apprenticeship Act* by the *Apprenticeship and Tradesmen's Qualification Act*. The new Act expanded the industrial training mandate of the department to encompass not only apprenticeship but also the more general domain of "manpower training." As a result of the expansion of its domain, the department introduced new programs and established a labour market research capacity.

"Supported by its own research branch, the Department of Labour presently appeared to be on the verge of a major thrust in vocational education.

The department was, in effect, laying claim to a clear alternative to [the Department of] Education's concept of vocational training" (Dupré *et al.* 1973, p. 76). The labour department was foiled in its plans largely because of the establishment of the colleges of applied arts and technology (community colleges) in 1966 by the education department. The colleges further cemented and expanded the role of provincial institutions in the delivery of training. The colleges grew quickly and by the 1980s had 90 campuses in 60 communities serving over 110,000 full-time, and close to 800,000 part-time, students (Premier's Council 1990, p. 57).

The existence of the two systems of providing training caused the emergence of competition between the departments responsible. The "conflict between Education and Labour was anything but an academic disagreement over pedagogical techniques. The two departments were in open competition for control of funds available for training" (Dupré *et al.* 1973, p. 81). In this competition, the labour department was hindered in that it did not have an organizational base in communities to serve clients to match the institutions funded by the Department of Education. The only organizational units of the labour department directly involved in training delivery, the local apprenticeship offices, were primarily regulatory offices.

In response to the competition between departments, the government commissioned an external study in 1971, headed by an academic, on organizational arrangements for training policy. The study recommended the transfer of all industrial training activities from the Department of Labour to the newly created Department of Colleges and Universities. The colleges and universities department had been carved from the Department of Education with responsibilities for postsecondary institutions. The transfer was to eliminate "undesirable competition and duplication ... because of the separation between" the institutions of the education department and the programs of the labour department while at the same time centralizing training policy (Crispo *et al.* 1972, p. 3). Under the new premier, William Davis, the government acted on the recommendation in 1972 to transfer all industrial training responsibilities to the Ministry of Colleges and Universities in 1972 (at this time in an unrelated development the titles of all departments were changed to "ministry").

The marriage of the institutional and industrial training proved to be a tumultuous one. The "bitter rivalry between labour market economists and educationalists within the government" did not disappear when brought under the same (ministry) roof (McFadyen 1994, p. 121). Between 1972 and 1985 the Industrial Training Branch (later named the Planning and Development Branch), with responsibility for industrial training, and the College Affairs Branch, with responsibility for the operating and capital grants to the colleges had "different roles and functions [which] ... inevitably led to the adoption of different priorities and perspectives. The College Affairs Branch possessed a greater sensitivity to the issues and problems faced by colleges, and gave priority to the institutional integrity of the colleges" (McFadyen 1994, p.122). The Planning and Development Branch, by contrast, had become "more concerned with the role of government in facilitating the smooth functioning of the labour market" (ibid.). From 1972 to 1985 the two branches were regularly combined in one division and then split and positioned in separate divisions within the Ministry of Colleges and Universities (MCU).

Further complicating matters, the Ministry of Labour (MoL) continued to exercise a role in training policy. The ministry's interest was motivated by its perception that industrial training, and labour market adjustment in general, were receiving insufficient attention by the colleges and universities ministry. The Ontario Manpower Commission was established in 1979 as a permanent part of the MoL, with responsibility for the general coordination and planning of training programs. The manpower commission also began to acquire responsibility for federal-provincial negotiations on training and obtained the lead role in the monitoring and evaluation of youth employment policy. In short, the commission was taking the role of a lead agency with responsibility for training and labour market adjustment policy, but without responsibility for the delivery of programs.

In 1982 the manpower commission began to report directly to the new Cabinet Committee on Manpower, chaired by the minister of labour, created in response to the increasing importance of labour market adjustment policy. The committee "represented a[n] ... attempt by the Ministry of Labour to re-establish its leadership role in the realm of active labour market policy" (ibid., p. 127).

By 1984, the manpower commission began to suggest, on the basis of evaluation studies it had conducted, that the delivery of training programs by colleges was ineffective. The colleges, the commission argued, failed to adequately respond to the needs of industry and labour. To remedy this state of affairs, the chair of the commission proposed that "It would seem ... appropriate to restructure the province's manpower and training responsibilities into a manpower division or ministry ... This appears to be the most obvious way of signalling and bringing about increased emphasis on the industrial training aspects of the overall question of manpower training (Wilson memorandum, 13 April, p. 5).

The increasing attention of policymakers to labour market adjustment in the 1980s was partly driven by high levels of youth unemployment. The entrance of large numbers of the baby-boom generation into the labour force during the recession of the early 1980s caused youth unemployment rates in Ontario to soar. Between 1975 and 1982 the unemployment rate for youth (ages 15-24) in Ontario hovered between 2.3 and 2.7 times that

**Table 1: Unemployment Rates (percent) for Ontario for Selected Years, 1956 to 1990 (selected age groups)**

| Year | Age Groups | | Ontario Total |
| --- | --- | --- | --- |
| | 15-19 years | 20-24 years | |
| 1956 | 4.3 | 3.2 | 2.4 |
| 1961 | 10.9 | 7.2 | 5.5 |
| 1966 | 6.9 | 3.2 | 2.5 |
| 1971 | 13.9 | 7.8 | 5.3 |
| 1976 | 14.7 | 8.8 | 6.2 |
| 1981 | 15.4 | 10.0 | 6.6 |
| 1982 | 19.7 | 15.6 | 9.8 |
| 1983 | 19.6 | 16.7 | 10.4 |
| 1984 | 17.3 | 13.5 | 9.1 |
| 1985 | 15.8 | 11.6 | 8.0 |
| 1986 | 13.2 | 10.5 | 7.0 |
| 1987 | 12.1 | 8.3 | 6.1 |
| 1988 | 10.0 | 7.0 | 5.0 |
| 1989 | 9.9 | 6.7 | 5.1 |
| 1990 | 12.2 | 9.3 | 6.3 |

Source: Ministry of Treasury and Economics (1986); Statistics Canada (1990).

of adults (ages 25-65). This ratio had not exceeded two during the previous decades. At the same time, labour market observers were beginning to predict that "present and future cohorts of Canadian youth will continue to experience unemployment problems" (Lowe and Krahn 1988, p. 58). As illustrated in Table 1, by 1983 the unemployment rates had reached unprecedented levels — 20 percent for ages 15-19; 17 percent for ages 20-24 — and were becoming a high-profile political issue. The opposition Liberal Party struck a Task Force on Jobs for Youth which toured the province and produced, in 1983, a report highly critical of government policies.

The escalation in youth unemployment levels, along with associated political pressures on the government during the early 1980s, resulted in three organizational responses. The first was the creation of a new agency, the Ontario Youth Secretariat, attached to the Ministry of Treasury and Economics to administer a variety of newly concocted youth employment initiatives. The second response was the ad hoc development of youth employment programs, such as Ontario Youth Start, Ontario Career Action, and Ontario Youth Corps by individual ministries, including MCU, the Ministry of Municipal Affairs and Housing, and others. Lastly, in mid-1984 the office of Ontario Youth Commissioner was created to coordinate the various initiatives and programs.

## THE POLITICAL IMPERATIVE

The birth of the Ministry of Skills Development (MSD) in 1985 was tied intimately to the political environment of the province. Since 1943 Ontario had been governed by a succession of long-serving Progressive Conservative premiers, the latest of which was Bill Davis. Before becoming premier, Davis had been minister of education for a decade and was responsible for the expansion of the colleges. Davis felt that demands on both industrial and institutional training could be accommodated within existing ministries and that no major organizational changes were required. As he expressed it, "industrial training was an educational experience" and therefore "there were no turf wars between ministries" because beginning with his tenure as premier in the early 1970s, one ministry (colleges and universities) was accountable for postsecondary "education in the broadest sense."

Davis stated that although there were some discussions during the later years of his tenure about the establishment of a new ministry mandated to deal with training, he "never contemplated a full fledged minister."

Davis' retirement announcement in September 1984 was the catalyst for a chain of profound events that would directly impact on youth and training policy. In early 1985, Frank Miller became the new leader of the Conservatives and premier. On 22 March 1985, three days before calling an election, Miller announced the creation of a new ministry: the MSD. According to the premier, the ministry was to rationalize "31 training programs administered by 12 different ministries and agencies" (Miller 1985, p. 16). The new organization was positioned not as an increase in government bureaucracy, but as a consolidation of existing services. Politically, the announcement of a new ministry allowed him to deflect criticisms from the opposition parties about the high youth unemployment rate.

The decision by Miller to create MSD involved no consultation with key Cabinet members or senior civil servants who learned of the ministry's creation only the day before the announcement was made public (Speirs 1986, pp. 93-94). There were no public consultations or any studies, other than the internal-to-government work of the manpower commission that preceded the decision. Miller's decision making is in contrast to the previous reorganization of the policy area in 1972, which was based on the recommendations of an independent commission.

The skills development ministry was established formally by Order-in-Council on 25 March 1985, the same day on which the provincial election was called. The Order-in-Council, which brought the agency to life, did not include a statement about the mandate of the new organization, listing only the programs to be transferred from other ministries. Miller appointed Ernie Eves as minister, and Blair Tully, a long-time civil servant with a background in central agencies, as deputy minister.

The May 1985 election results failed to provide any party with a majority of the seats in the Legislature. Under Miller, the Conservatives continued to form the government for several weeks after the election. Phil Gillies, who was appointed skills development minister days after the May election to replace Eves (in a Cabinet shuffle), introduced legislation (Bill 9) in the Legislature to establish the ministry in statute and affirm the executive order of the Cabinet. The installation weeks later of a minority Liberal government with David Peterson as premier meant that Bill 9 was not called for second reading and the MSD continued to rely on the Order-in-Council as the basis for its mission. The long-term effects on the new ministry of the tumultuous pre- and post-election periods are discussed in some detail later. Its creation on the eve of the end of decades of Conservative rule did, however, immediately raise questions about the legitimacy of the organization under a new regime.

The Liberal government operated with the support of the New Democratic Party (NDP) under a public, formal agreement, the Liberal-New Democratic Accord, which specified the broad policy agenda of the minority administration. With respect to labour market adjustment policy, the accord merely stated that the minority government would "introduce programs to create employment and training opportunities for young people" (Liberals and NDP 1985). The initial list of ministerial responsibilities by the Peterson government failed to mention MSD, noting only that Gregory Sorbara was "Minister of Colleges and Universities (Skills Training, Youth Year)" (Premier's Office 1985). Miller's rash decision to create the skills development ministry had caught the Liberals unprepared. During the formation of the Peterson Cabinet some of his advisors argued for "an office of skills development" within the Ministry of Education (MoEd) rather than a separate ministry in order to control the size of Cabinet, while others recommended a new ministry of employment and skills training.

The inability to resolve the status of the MSD along with the desire of Sorbara and senior bureaucrats to resuscitate the newly born agency led to the hiring of an external consultant to evaluate the need for the ministry. The consultant's report to the Premier's Office concluded that "the most effective administrative mechanism to deal with skills training at this time would be a strongly-mandated, stand alone ministry" (confidential report, September 1985). The report emphasized that such a ministry

> will require a very high level strategic planning capacity. In this light, and in view of the clear need for sorting out and streamlining the multiplicity of advisory committees ... the Ontario Manpower Commission should be dissolved, and in its stead, a Province of Ontario Training Board should be established to act as a dynamic, forward-looking advisory board (to the Minister). It should be chaired by ... eminent individuals and assisted by high calibre professionals (ibid.)

The recommendation to retain the skills development ministry was accepted by the premier, and the ministry's independent status confirmed in the fall of 1985 with Sorbara as minister. The centre made no effort to decree a mandate for the new organization. Indeed, a senior advisor to Peterson noted at the time "that giving MSD its own 'stand-alone' department raises all kinds of problems re MCU's future. Are we saying we should have three ministries where two existed before?" (confidential memo, 30 September 1985). The recommendation to establish a corporatist advisory board was not acted on by the new government, although the idea was to re-emerge later in the decade and find fruition in the 1990s under a different political regime.

Davis had been firm during his tenure as premier that industrial and institutional training were inseparable and that therefore one ministry would have responsibility for both. Peterson did not have a clear position on labour market policy, as events would show. Unlike Davis, Peterson had no background in education or training issues, or experience as a Cabinet member; while his advisors were also unfamiliar with this policy area. In recalling his years as premier he noted "the struggle to come up with efficiencies" in training policy and the need "to try different approaches to see which one works best ... since any way you organize government is wrong."

The Liberals' long absence from power meant that they had little experience in the management of the machinery of government which encompassed two dozen ministries, countless agencies, and 80,000 civil servants. White (1993) illustrates the extent to which this was true in his research on the transition in 1985 from the Conservative to the Liberal governments. He writes that a "senior Liberal staff member recalled, early in the transition, trying to figure out the structure and operation of the cabinet by looking through the government telephone book" (1993, p. 116). He also writes that one central figure in Peterson's office "indicated that in retrospect, more thought should have been given to the structures of government. Another subsequently came to realize that, as a group, the Liberals — ministers and top staff — had only limited understanding of the dynamics of large organizations, how and why they work and the nature and significance of corporate culture" (ibid., p. 135). Fortunately, the lack of expertise on the part of Liberals in governing was mitigated somewhat by the policy agenda negotiated for the minority government between the Liberals and NDP.

During its first months the skills development ministry had two discordant mandates. The first, provided by Miller at the time he announced the ministry's creation, was to: (i) work in partnership with business and labour as well as with the Ministries of Education, Colleges and Universities, Industry and Trade, Labour, Community and Social Services and Treasury and Economics to design a comprehensive skills development policy; (ii) ensure that youth initiatives are linked to training and employment; (iii) rationalize the division of responsibility between Ottawa and Ontario; and (iv) refine existing programs as well as streamline budgetary and delivery mechanisms for institutional and on-the-job training (Miller 1985, pp. 16-19; MSD, News Release, 11 June 1985, p. 3).

The second mandate as outlined in Bill 9 was to upgrade skills to enhance the employability of individuals; contribute to economic growth by helping employers achieve their skills development goals; improve access to training and employment opportunities for employed and unemployed individuals, including persons with special needs and targeted groups; coordinate institutional and on-the-job training programs; and heighten awareness of, and appreciation for, the economic and social benefits of improved skills training and employment mobility.

The first mandate is specific and pointed the organization toward strategic economic policy, highlighting youth unemployment and the role of the federal government. Of note is the explicit reference to the ministry's coordination role vis-à-vis other ministries in developing policy. The second iteration of the mandate (Bill 9) has greater emphasis on social policy illustrated by references to "persons with special needs" and the "social benefits of training." References to youth and the federal government are found in the first mandate statement, but not the second. The differences in the two mandates — drafted by the same government — suggest that there was uncertainty about what should be the prime functions of the new ministry. The shift in mandate also reflects the results of the election which saw the political pendulum shift from the right to the centre.

Once the Liberal government took office, there was no formal revision to the main objectives of MSD as stated in Bill 9. In 1986, Sorbara reintroduced the unaltered bill in the Legislature, which again was not called for second reading by the government before the 1987 election. By default, the objectives in the failed Bill 9 became the official, yet unapproved, mandate of MSD. The curious failure to call the Bill to second reading suggests that the Liberals remained unsure about the necessity of the agency and its mandate. For the ministry, the lack of formal endorsement generated continued uncertainty about its mission, if not its future.

During the political changes and uncertainty of 1985, Tully and his officials worked to establish and consolidate MSD as an organization by negotiating the transfer of staff and resources from other ministries and agencies, including the absorption of the manpower commission. The process was made particularly frustrating by the uncertainty in the larger political environment, and the turnover of ministers.

In obtaining resources from the colleges and universities ministry, MSD had been outmaneouvred even prior to its existence. Notwithstanding the secrecy surrounding the announcement by Miller of the ministry's birth in the spring of 1985, officials in the postsecondary ministry had prepared for such an eventuality. Six weeks before the announcement, the colleges and universities ministry was reorganized by senior management "because priority must at this time be given to the administration of the college system" (Benson memorandum, 8 February 1985, p. 2). The reorganization transferred staff to the college administration function of the ministry (which was not transferred to MSD) from the industrial training function (which subsequently was transferred to MSD). For the new skills development ministry the hasty MCU reorganization meant that it received fewer resources for its industrial training mandate than would otherwise have been the case. The reorganization reduced the negative impact on MCU of the skills development ministry's creation, which was nonetheless significant. Of the $305 million of resources transferred to MSD from other ministries, more than 55 percent came from the colleges and universities ministry.

By early 1986 all the organizational pieces of the new training ministry were in place, allowing Tully, the deputy minister, to announce the completion of "the process of consolidation and rationalization which began with the merging of resources from six different provincial ministries" (memorandum, 9 April 1986). He noted that "[w]hile there has been much uncertainty over the past year ... I am pleased to say that we are well on our way" (ibid.).

The ministry's basic structure, illustrated in Figure 1, remained largely unchanged from 1986 to 1990, and was comprised of three major divisions: (i) Policy and Development, (ii) Skills Training, and (iii) Finance and Administration. The figure also identifies the parentage of each of the branches of the new ministry. The Skills Training, and Policy and Development divisions were each headed by an assistant deputy minister. The Finance and Administration Division, headed by an executive director, provided management, information, and financial support services.

The policy division had responsibility for policy and program development, evaluation, and federal-provincial relations. The division was a mix of young newly hired staff with backgrounds in economics and policy analysis, and staff transferred from other ministries. Coming from the labour ministry was the labour market research group (the core of the manpower commission) comprised of labour market economists; while the small federal-provincial relations group came from the colleges and universities ministry. The skills training division was the operational arm of the agency. All staff in the division were transferred from other ministries and agencies. Initially the division had three branches — Apprenticeship, Youth, and Training Services — corresponding to the major program clusters.

The consequences of the very early history of MSD were both positive and negative. On the negative side, the ministry was hastily established without a formal consultation process either inside or outside the government. Key stakeholders had no opportunity to buy into the new organization and were unprepared for its arrival. This would prove problematic given the political and bureaucratic turmoil that was to follow the defeat of the Conservatives later in 1985. Second, MSD did not have a charter document enshrined in statute which outlined its *raison d'être*, leaving unclear the priorities of the agency. Third, MSD experienced severe political uncertainty and change in its initial few months. When the Liberals came into power, some new Liberal decisionmakers saw the skills development ministry as the work and progeny of the previous government. Consequently, the ministry had to justify its existence to the Liberals who had played no role in its recent birth.

On the positive side, MSD did secure the endorsement from the new government for its existence and mission. The Liberals recognized that the organization was a useful vehicle to address the youth unemployment

**Figure 1: Organizational Chart of the Ministry of Skills Development**

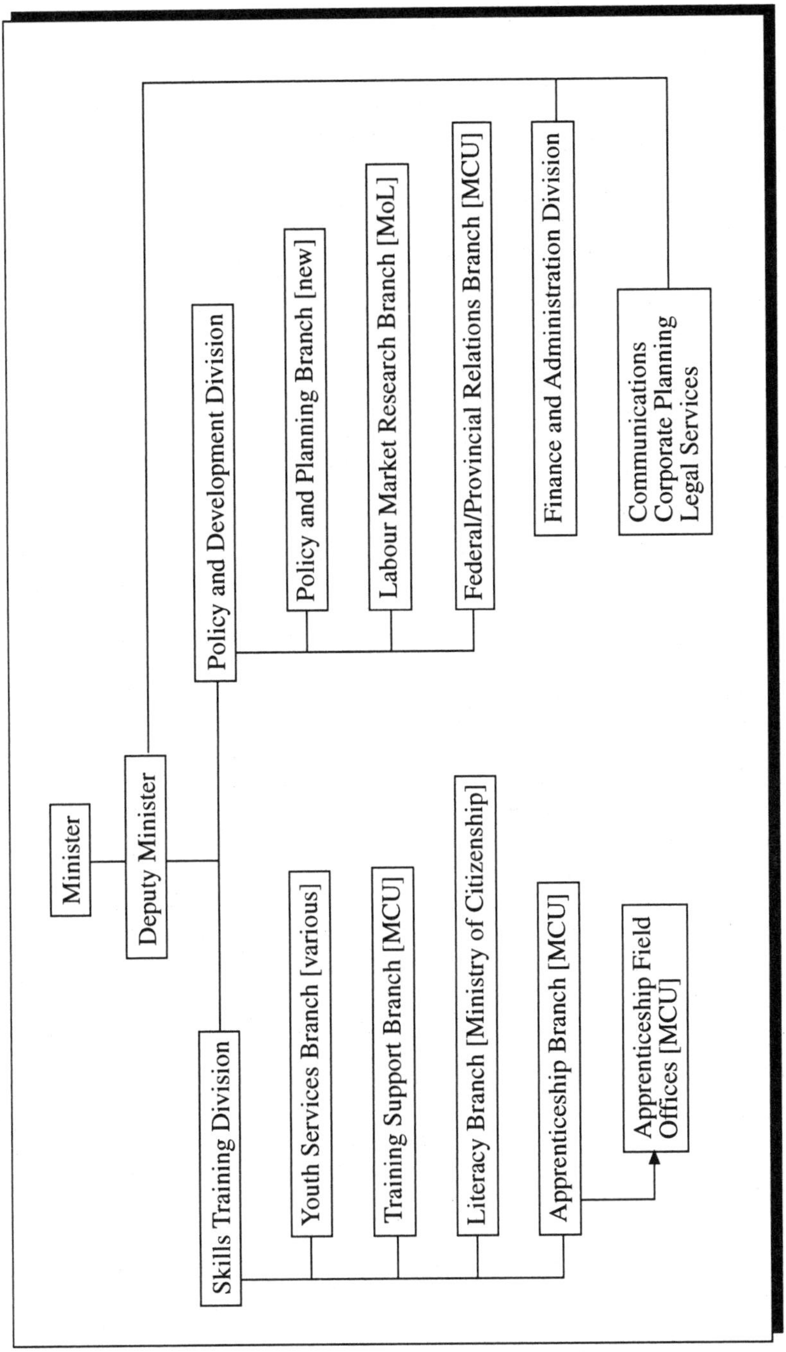

Minister

Deputy Minister

Policy and Development Division
- Policy and Planning Branch [new]
- Labour Market Research Branch [MoL]
- Federal/Provincial Relations Branch [MCU]

Finance and Administration Division
- Communications
- Corporate Planning
- Legal Services

Skills Training Division
- Youth Services Branch [various]
- Training Support Branch [MCU]
- Literacy Branch [Ministry of Citizenship]
- Apprenticeship Branch [MCU]
- Apprenticeship Field Offices [MCU]

problem on which the party had taken a strong stand in the election campaign. Second, policymakers saw the organization as a solution to the long-standing conflict between industrial and institutional training and as a way to react to federal policies. Third, the unsettled political environment and the new government's preoccupation with meeting the terms of the Liberal-NDP accord provided the ministry with time away from the limelight to establish and prove itself.

## EARLY SUCCESSES

Between 1985 and 1987 the agency's accomplishments were two-fold. The first was a partial rationalization of training programs for youth. The FUTURES program, announced in October 1985, replaced and consolidated six programs for hard-to-employ youth ages 16-24 both out of work and out of school. The program provided a range of services, including employment preparation and counselling, work placement, on-the-job training and financial support for educational upgrading. The FUTURES program was delivered, under contract for MSD, by two sets of delivery agencies: colleges and community-based social services agencies. By quickly forging a single program that removed some of the inconsistencies, gaps, and duplications in existing programs for youth the ministry sought to meet the requirements of the Liberal-NDP accord.

FUTURES became the major component of MSD's services for youth, comprising somewhat more than one-quarter of the ministry's expenditures. Notwithstanding the consolidation that FUTURES represented, the ministry was still left with programs (such as Environmental Youth Corps) that provided wage subsidies for employers to hire students, summer employment programs, and a program providing loans for young entrepreneurs.

The ministry's second major initiative, with the grandiose name of Ontario's Training Strategy, was approved by Cabinet in June 1986 and publicly announced in September. The strategy was to be the adult training complement to the FUTURES program for youth as well as the province's response to the federal government's recent Canadian Jobs Strategy which sought to strengthen industrial training (McFadyen 1994). However, the provincial strategy did not achieve the same degree of program consolidation as did the FUTURES initiative in youth policy.

The strategy was composed of five, oft unconnected, components. The first was a training consulting service for businesses using colleges as the delivery structure. The MSD's administrative leadership had initially hoped, as one official expressed it, "to build up a series of offices across the province to fly its own flag" delivering and coordinating programs. However, two conditions forced the ministry to retain the colleges as delivery agents: first, the imperative on the ministry and Cabinet to placate the colleges by not taking resources away from them; and second, the substantial cost of establishing such a delivery structure, when the colleges already delivered some of the same services.

The second component of the strategy were grants for businesses to train employees. The third component was the Ontario Basic Skills program which funded literacy, numeracy, computer, life, and other related skills courses for individuals over 25 years of age. The fourth component was the Trades Updating program funding courses for workers in skilled trades whose employment was changing due to technology, increasing specialization, and shifting job markets. The above four components of the strategy were all delivered through the colleges.

The final component of the strategy was the creation of an institute for skills training which eventually became the Ontario Training Corporation. The arm's-length agency was established in 1988 to develop training products and services for the private sector. It played no major role in labour market adjustment policy and is therefore not discussed in detail.

Although all components of the strategy were billed to be new, comprising a comprehensive labour market adjustment policy, in reality the majority were renamed, expanded, and otherwise altered services that MSD already provided. Unlike the FUTURES program there was no rationalization or consolidation evident in the initiative. The completely new components were the trades updating program and the establishment of the institute for skills training, but these accounted for only 10 percent of total expenditures. The budget for the five services was $100 million representing about one-quarter of the ministry's total budget.

The programs under the strategy represent the majority of the second program cluster of MSD — namely industrial and pre-employment training programs for adults. These programs were heterogeneous serving several distinct groups: adults who needed basic employment-related skills, highly specialized workers requiring upgraded skills, and employers seeking to finance training.

The third program area of the ministry, apprenticeship, proved to be the most resistant to change. The apprenticeship branch came from MCU and had been a part of the labour ministry prior to 1971 with a long history and a culture that involved close linkages with employers and unions. Apprenticeship was MSD's most complex program involving employers, trade unions, colleges, and the federal government. Under the apprenticeship program companies absorbed the cost of workplace training and paid the wages of apprentices. Unions provided additional training for apprentices in some sectors such as the construction trades. The colleges provided the classroom, or in-school, portion of training for apprentices which was primarily funded by the federal government. MSD bore the cost of administering the program by providing the monitoring, enforcement, testing, and certification functions through its 27 field offices across the province. The ministry also "topped up" the in-class portion of training beyond the federal contribution. The delivery and administration of the apprenticeship program involved one-third of MSD's staff, but only 15 percent of its total budget.

Only in the apprenticeship program did the ministry's staff interact directly with the ultimate clients; the colleges, community groups, and other agencies delivered all other programs. In fact, a very high proportion of the ministry's expenditures involved transfer payments to other organizations. Of the $385 million in annual expenditures of the operations division, 93 percent were transfer payments (MSD 1989/90).

As part of the pre-election preparations in 1987, MSD proposed three new initiatives: expanding the apprenticeship program, Help Centres, and the Transition program. Peterson announced these initiatives as part of the summer 1987 election campaign. The Transition program provided laid-off workers over the age of 45 years with monetary credits to purchase training to allow them to stay in the labour force. The program, and its specific target group — older, recently laid-off workers — represented a shift in the ministry's programming. The program involved the agency for the first time with clients (laid-off workers) who were primarily being served by the labour ministry through its plant closure and employment adjustment functions.

The Transition program was small initially ($1 million per year), but began to grow with the increasing number of layoffs in the province during the late 1980s, especially in the manufacturing sector. Help Centres were community-based agencies, funded by MSD, providing employment counselling and training referral for unemployed workers. The Transition program and the Help Centres comprised the fourth distinct set of MSD programs; namely programs for laid-off and recently unemployed workers.

## RELATIONS WITH OTHER AGENCIES

As described above, the activities of the skills development ministry modified political and policy relationships in the labour market adjustment field. The ministry existed in a policy area already populated by other older and/ or larger agencies whose (re)actions played a critical role in MSD's ultimate demise.

Some decisionmakers in central agencies and line ministries came to believe, early in the new ministry's life, that its domain greatly overlapped those of other ministries. Their belief was, as one deputy minister stated, that "although differentiating between the mandate of MSD and MCU was possible on paper it did not work in the real world." There were several reasons for the overlap in domain. The fact that the Legislature did not enact the MSD Act (Bill 9) meant that the ministry never acquired a founding document or charter which formally defined its mandate. Without a ratified mission, other ministries had reasonable cause to believe that MSD was, or would be, following objectives detrimental to the well-being of their clients, delivery agents, and stakeholders. In one case, described below, MSD threatened the very existence of another ministry. Sorbara's political inexperience may have contributed to the inattention paid to interministerial relationships. He was first elected to the Legislature in the 1985 election and immediately thrust into Cabinet. As well, clear signals from the centre (as had been the case during the Davis years) could have arbitrarily drawn boundaries between ministries; however, the new premier and his Cabinet did not do so during the ministry's early years.

A second cause for the overlap in domain between the skills development ministry and other ministries was the nature of labour market adjustment policy. The policy area involved a diverse group of stakeholders, business, labour, and colleges, who had close linkages with other ministries and the federal government. For example, although the skills ministry was to be responsible for the administration and regulation of apprenticeship, aspects of the instruction and learning component were provided by the colleges and funded by the federal government.

Third, from birth, MSD was torn between having primarily an economic focus or a social policy focus. One assistant deputy minister at MSD noted that they "were neither fish nor fowl." The agency was unable to determine whether its goals principally lay in aiding economic growth or in helping disadvantaged individuals. In other words, should the ministry's programs target individuals who would take best advantage of government training funds to become better trained, or should they target the most disadvantaged with little labour market attachment? MSD was never provided with unambiguous direction from the centre on this question and it thus continued to haunt the organization.

The ministry's administrative leadership in 1985 and 1986, Tully, and Les Horswill, assistant deputy minister of the policy division, both initially conceived of the organization as a labour market and business-driven ministry supporting economic competitiveness. They viewed MSD's focus as "training for competitiveness, not for social issues." This view as consistent with Miller's initial vision of the agency as supporting the private sector, Sorbara's own background as a solicitor in the private sector, and with Tully and Horswill's own training as economists. According to one central agency official, because of "Tully's interests and background, the ministry was initially set on a course which ignored pressures to help the disadvantaged in society." However, the social policy ministers in the Liberal Cabinet began to look to MSD's skills training programs as the solution to their problems: poverty, rising social assistance caseloads, and employment equity.

Not surprisingly, domain overlap was greatest between MSD and MCU, as the two ministries had many of the same clients. Not only was the new skills development ministry struggling to clarify its mission, so was the restructured, and downsized, colleges and universities ministry. In the creation of the training agency, MCU had ceded responsibility for the administration of apprenticeship, other industrial training programs, and federal-provincial relations. Consequently, MCU's domain had been significantly limited to a ministry of institutions, rather than a ministry of postsecondary education and training. Most staff at MCU perceived no value in a separate ministry that would, in their view, do what their ministry had been doing for more than a decade. A postsecondary ministry executive stated that "there was a very high degree of cynicism at MCU about the new ministry and we were not at all supportive of MSD."

The overlap and conflict between the two ministries centred on the role and funding of the colleges. The fears of MCU staff were two-fold, and were well-known to MSD staff. The first fear was that the new ministry would not be supportive of the agencies of MCU (the colleges) ultimately seeking to supplant them as providers of training. The second concern at the colleges and universities ministry was that MSD was taking advantage of the MCU resources made available to colleges. A manager at MSD explained that "MCU was in a difficult position by the fact that we purchased specific courses from colleges and paid the direct costs. MCU felt that it was subsidizing these courses by funding the indirect costs: buildings and equipment."

Lastly, the colleges and universities ministry had the most to lose from a successful MSD, which could ultimately raise questions about the need for MCU's continued existence. An effective training ministry might well argue that it required a more direct relationship with colleges necessitating the transfer of that responsibility from MCU. A successful skills development ministry would also make it obvious that MCU had been inept in managing labour market adjustment policy prior to 1985.

To protect the colleges from MSD, the postsecondary education ministry moved to strengthen its domain and relationship with the colleges so as to "freeze out" its competitor. For example, over a span of four years from 1985-89 the deputy ministers of MCU and MSD did not schedule a single joint visit to a college. This is remarkable because the colleges bitterly complained, to both organizations, about the lack of cooperation between them. The reasons for the lack of joint visits are unclear and it is unknown whether overtures were made and rejected by one of the ministries. In any event, such a state of affairs is evidence of the bureaucratic warfare that existed.

Another element of the MCU strategy was a ministerial directive to colleges in 1986 requiring that each college submit an annual strategic plan. The requirement came about because there were concerns in government that colleges were not sufficiently accountable for their activities. Furthermore, in 1987, the colleges were required to conduct ongoing operational reviews of their activities and report the results to the colleges and universities ministry. Both the annual reports and operational reviews illustrate how the postsecondary ministry acted to increase its interaction with, and overview of, colleges just after the creation of the skills development ministry. There is no direct evidence to suggest that the intent of the new policies was to undermine the new training ministry. MCU officials stated that the timing of these events was coincidental, but did not disagree that the new requirements served to enhance the existing MCU-colleges bond at the expense of MSD. The coincidence seems particularly convenient and it is likely that postsecondary education officials deliberately overstated the need for increased accountability as a means to justify its new hands-on relationship with the colleges.

Knowledge about the interministry tension became widely known and Sorbara, as the minister of both departments, was forced to discuss it in the Legislature. In reply to a question from the Opposition he stated:

> you expressed some concern with respect to senior bureaucracy warfare [between MSD and MCU]. While it is an interesting issue to bring up ... I think any warfare, to the extent that it exists, is dramatically exaggerated. Frankly, I think any disagreement between ministries probably arises out of concern with the letter of intent ... There were some — not at the senior levels — who would have preferred it [MSD] to be back in the Ministry of Colleges and Universities ... As minister, I realize the importance of establishing ongoing linkages at all levels of the bureaucracy ... I think that any suggestion of warfare is the reflection of one or two individuals ... *(Hansard*, Standing Committee on General Government, 5 February 1986, p. G-433).

Outside observers also commented on tensions between MSD and MCU. One noted that "there is competition between these ministries and that ... colleges could well find themselves ground between these millstones" (Pitman 1986, p. 35).

## MULTIPLE AND CONTESTED CLIENTS

In the absence of an agreed-upon domain, the skills development ministry experienced difficulties in deciding who its clients were and what programs it should provide for them. The ministry had a set of disparate clients; for example, its own publications listed: (i) unemployed youth, (ii) employers and unions, (iii) employed and unemployed adults, (iv) community-based organizations, (v) summer students, (vi) recently unemployed adults 45 years and older, and (vii) colleges (MSD 1988*a*). The problem was that, in the words of a MSD deputy minister, "none of the ministry's clients were primarily its own." He went on to add that the lack of its own constituency was the ministry's "great dilemma."

The lack of an exclusive set of clients meant that MSD had to engage in a great deal of interorganizational interaction in almost all aspects of its activities, unlike a ministry such as the colleges and universities. For example, MCU introduced the new accountability requirements for the colleges without consulting other ministries. Without groups directly dependent upon MSD, the ministry's basis for external legitimacy and support were limited. Moreover, that few MSD staff (rather than college and community agency staff) were located in the field meant that clients were often not even aware when ministry programs were serving them. As a result, it was a formidable task for the ministry to develop a grass-roots constituency which could advocate on its behalf.

Most important for the new organization were the two education ministries (MCU and the MoEd), the labour ministry, the industry ministry, and the social services ministry, many of whose clients were attempting to enter the labour force. Reflecting their different mandates, there is considerable variation in terms of staff and expenditures between ministries as illustrated in Tables 2 and 3.

The tables together illustrate that there is no necessary connection between the budget of a ministry and the number of staff in that ministry. The labour ministry had a comparatively small budget but a relatively large number of staff, in keeping with its primary function of regulating the workplace and labour market. On the other hand, the MCU had a comparatively large budget but relatively few staff, in keeping with its function as a transfer payment agent for universities, colleges, and students. MSD,

## Table 2: Expenditures for Selected Ministries, 1979 to 1991 (millions of dollars)

| Year | MCU | MCSS | Ministry MoEd | MITT | MoL | MSD |
|------|-----|------|------|------|-----|-----|
| 1979 | 1,371 | 1,228 | 2,391 | 60 | 34 | -- |
| 1980 | 1,446 | 1,342 | 2,563 | 68 | 41 | -- |
| 1981 | 1,542 | 1,528 | 2,604 | 81 | 51 | -- |
| 1982 | 1,670 | 1,770 | 3,045 | 89 | 59 | -- |
| 1983 | 1,883 | 2,123 | 3,161 | 149 | 67 | -- |
| 1984 | 2,035 | 2,402 | 3,434 | 76 | 73 | -- |
| 1985 | 2,101 | 2,605 | 3,219 | 80 | 74 | -- |
| 1986 | 2,063 | 2,863 | 3,380 | 82 | 76 | 392 |
| 1987 | 2,254 | 3,285 | 3,937 | 197 | 97 | 405 |
| 1988 | 2,391 | 3,775 | 4,447 | 137 | 107 | 385 |
| 1989 | 2,668 | 4,312 | 5,111 | 156 | 119 | 402 |
| 1990 | 2,731 | 5,062 | 5,321 | 208 | 133 | 415 |
| 1991 | 2,861 | 6,442 | 5,526 | 267 | 164 | 243 |

Key: MCU  = Ministry of Colleges and Universities
MCSS = Ministry of Community and Social Services
MoEd = Ministry of Education
MITT = Ministry of Industry, Trade and Technology
MoL  = Ministry of Labour
MSD  = Ministry of Skills Development

Note: The data in the table is presented by fiscal year. Therefore, the data for 1979 is from 1 April 1979 to 31 March 1980 and so forth for all other years.

Source: Ontario. *Public Accounts* (annual), various years.

prior to its decline in 1990, had a budget larger than the labour and industry ministries, but smaller than the education and social services ministries; while the number of its staff was greater than MCU, but smaller than the other ministries. In short, in terms of staff and total expenditures the skills development ministry was a mid-sized ministry.

The five ministries were also quite different in their histories, corporate cultures, and ultimately in their reactions to MSD and its successor. The Ministry of Education was one of the oldest ministries in the government and one that enjoyed a high level of prestige in the 1960s and 1970s under

**Table 3: Staff Levels for Selected Ministries, 1989 to 1991**

| | | | Ministry | | | |
|---|---|---|---|---|---|---|
| Year | MCU | MCSS | MoEd | MITT | MoL | MSD |
| 1989 | 389 | 11,247 | 2,219 | 787 | 1,866 | 677 |
| 1990 | 410 | 11,185 | 2,208 | 760 | 1,806 | 620 |
| 1991 | 338 | 11,124 | 2,352 | 733 | 1,902 | 459 |

Key: MCU = Ministry of Colleges and Universities
MCSS = Ministry of Community and Social Services
MoEd = Ministry of Education
MITT = Ministry of Industry, Trade and Technology
MoL = Ministry of Labour
MSD = Ministry of Skills Development

Notes: 1. The number of staff includes both full-time and part-time staff.
2. The data in the tables is presented by fiscal year. Therefore, the data for 1989 is from 1 April 1989 to 31 March 1990 and so forth for all other years.

Source: Management Board of Cabinet, *Expenditure Estimates*, Vol. 2. various years.

Davis. In addition to developing curricula and related guidelines the ministry provided funding for school boards. The paramount professional group within the ministry was comprised of staff who were school teachers and who now developed curricula and provided advice to the school boards. As a result, until the mid-1980s there were few officials in high-level positions in the ministry not drawn from the school system.

The strong values surrounding the provision of public education, and the various institutionalized and powerful stakeholders of the ministry made changes in policy slow and difficult to achieve. By the mid-1980s the ministry was increasingly criticized as being too insular and isolated from the changes occurring in society and for not being sufficiently proactive about the high rate of drop outs and the problem of illiteracy.

The Ministry of Colleges and Universities had always been strongly linked with the other education ministry, having been carved from it in the 1970s. The connection between the two ministries was strengthened by the fact that secondary-school graduates are the largest source of students for the institutions of MCU, and that school teachers are trained in those institutions. The culture and mandate at the postsecondary ministry was in many ways an extension of that at its sister ministry, which is not surprising given their genealogy. The number of institutions served by the postsecondary ministry was small: 24 colleges and 15 universities. The colleges, as Crown corporations under the aegis of the ministry, were more closely tied to the ministry (for program approval, appointments to boards of governors, etc.) than were the more autonomous universities.

Unlike MoEd there was no formal curriculum-development function at MCU, leaving the transfer of funds (capital and operating) to the institutions and grants/loans to students as the prime function. Although the ministry had no curriculum policy function, the formula for the transfer of funds to the institutions was often employed as a thinly disguised policy tool. By the mid-1980s the ministry was under increasing pressure to ensure that the postsecondary institutions respond more effectively to societal demands and government policies.

The Ministry of Labour was quite different from both education ministries in terms of its organizational culture. The ministry had a broader legislative, regulatory, and mediation (between business and labour) function than either of the education ministries. The issues at the labour ministry were often immediate, controversial, and legalistic, relating to labour relations/disputes, occupational/industrial health and safety, and worker compensation/rehabilitation. MoL had a large number of stakeholders in the community with whom it consulted and interacted. In some cases, the key stakeholders (business and labour) had conflicting views (e.g., on the level of the minimum wage) which the agency mediated. The ministry had a much larger community presence than either of the education ministries. In the 1980s it had 85 field offices across Ontario while MoEd had but a handful, and MCU none at all. The field offices of the labour ministry meant that the ministry had a significant number of its own staff stationed throughout Ontario and in contact with members of the public, as well as business and labour groups.

The ministry's staff was much more heterogeneous than that at either of the education agencies, with a significant number having experience with community agencies and the private sector. One important professional group within MoL — in addition to legal and regulatory officials — was the labour market economists. A problem-solving technique often used at the ministry was to launch a commission, such as the Ontario Manpower Commission discussed earlier, to gather information and to use the results to bring, often antagonistic, stakeholders to consensus. MoL traditionally viewed itself as the principal ministry dealing with labour market adjustment issues and the only ministry effectively able to broker the views of both business and labour. By the mid-1980s the ministry — as exemplified by the creation of the manpower commission — perceived that skills training, as a labour market adjustment tool, was working poorly.

The final agency whose mandate pertained to labour market adjustment policy was the Ministry of Industry, Trade and Technology. However, the ministry traditionally had not seen labour market adjustment policy as part of its economic development function, reflecting the low level of interest in this issue by its major client group — business. The department's role in active labour market policy, and particularly training, would remain miniscule during the 1980s and 1990s.

Ironically, the group most dependent on MSD were the colleges, the self-governing agencies of the postsecondary ministry that delivered many training programs and services to businesses and individuals. Colleges, therefore, would be expected to be a major supporter of the skills development ministry, especially since funds from MSD represented about 25 percent of college budgets (comprising the largest component after funds received from MCU). Although the skills development ministry was composed of many former MCU staff, colleges did not naturally or automatically see MSD as an ally. The opposite, in fact, occurred with colleges coming to fear the training ministry. A college president stated that "MSD was not interested in the colleges" and that "from the point of view of colleges, the ministry was slanted against them." Although colleges continued to interact with many of the same individuals at the skills development ministry who had previously been at MCU, these individuals were responsible for industrial training programs which happened to purchase services provided by colleges. The programs, however, did not inexorably have to employ the colleges, but could obtain some of the same services from private vocational schools, secondary schools, and community-based agencies.

MSD policy staff, for the most part, saw colleges as delivery agents for training programs that the ministry was forced to utilize; they were instruments rather than clients. The colleges, representing institutional training, were seen by policymakers as having serious weaknesses, such as being slow to respond to the needs of the labour market and having high costs due to union contracts. Indeed, the inadequacy of the colleges as providers of training had been a prime reason for the genesis of the organization in the first place.

The administrative leadership of the MSD had considered, but rejected, establishing a separate delivery system as part of the Ontario Training Strategy in 1986. Nevertheless, senior officials continued to believe, as one stated, that "using the colleges was the wrong thing to do because it was an institutional response ... and business clients did not want to deal with institutions." While the training ministry was stuck with colleges as prime delivery agencies, it began to alter the service delivery relationship. Beginning in 1986, colleges no longer received block funding for the provision of industrial training services, but were required to enter into fee-for-service contracts with the ministry.

From the perspective of the colleges, the change was significant. They, like the universities, were accustomed to receiving block grants for their activities without the itemized accountability that MSD began to impose. The formula (enrolment driven) financing system used by MCU was hands-off from the point of view of the colleges; the MSD financing system was administratively demanding. For programs funded by MSD, colleges were required to complete additional paperwork and itemize many costs, while some colleges felt that the fee schedule was inadequate causing them to lose money in delivering services for the ministry.

In developing its policies, MSD was faced with an overlapping domain and multiple and contested clients. Not surprisingly, its programs were, as described by one assistant deputy minister, "a collection of unconnected services." The uncoordinated nature of programs was a natural result of the disparate clients being served by the programs, and the variety of delivery agencies. The majority of programs, with the exception of apprenticeship, met only a fraction of any client's training needs. The ministry did not itself create this fragmentation; it was inherent in the policy field and existed before the ministry's arrival. Nevertheless, the fragmentation became MSD's problem.

An example of the niche nature of MSD's programs is the Transition program that served older laid-off workers. The labour ministry had statutory requirements relating to plant closures and its staff was required to be at the site of lay-offs to assist management and workers. Staff of the labour ministry felt that their organization should have programs for laid-off workers, rather than MSD, so that one ministry could effectively meet the labour market adjustment needs of laid-off workers. Not surprisingly, MSD's new program caused friction between the two organizations, such as when MSD refused to reduce the age limit (to below 45 years) for clients of the Transition program as demanded by the labour ministry.

A second characteristic of MSD's programs was that the majority were delivered by third parties, especially the colleges, rather than by ministry staff. The college staff who delivered MSD programs were employed by the colleges, not MSD, and felt little allegiance to the ministry. Information on program delivery, such as overlap, underspending, client feedback, and so forth did not reach MSD as quickly as might have been the case had programs been delivered directly. One skills development ministry manager responsible for collecting program information noted that "there were problems getting data from the colleges in a timely manner, since they were not used to reporting quickly."

Some of the services provided by MSD were for government clients rather than for the public. Most important among these was the negotiation with the federal government for the purchase of training courses from the colleges. On behalf of the Ontario government, the ministry entered into a new three-year agreement with the federal government in 1986. The federal government was determined to curtail funding to colleges in keeping with its policy of reducing funding for institutional training. In negotiating with the federal government, MSD was in the awkward position of trying to obtain the best deal for the institutional training system being administered primarily by MCU. MSD staff felt, in the words of one official, "that no better deal was possible given the priorities of the federal government." The agreement entailed a decrease of funds to colleges and caused, in the words of a senior MSD participant, "blood and accusation to be hurled at the ministry from some colleges." Colleges, as one MSD executive related, "saw us as not being able to win money from Ottawa, when in the 1970s it was easy to do so."

That the ministry negotiated what colleges (and others, such as Opposition party critics) saw as an inferior agreement for Ontario (and its institutions) increased the initial distrust and bitterness between MSD and MCU. Over time, in the late 1980s, when the federal-provincial agreement proved not to be as detrimental for the colleges as first expected, the feelings lessened somewhat. Staff from the colleges and universities ministry, however, continued to believe that MSD was not effectively defending the interests of the colleges against the federal government.

The spending pattern of the FUTURES program illustrated another problem that MSD encountered early in its life. FUTURES was initially comprised of employment preparation services for youth that were already in the labour force but unemployed. The core of the program was 16 weeks of on-the-job training delivered by the employer, but subsidized by the ministry. A year and a half after the program was introduced, the MSD returned to Cabinet with what it called a "bold program shift." The shift was to expand eligibility for the program to part-time students due to less than anticipated demand for the program.

The need to expand the pool of potential FUTURES clients made the ministry appear to be out of touch with labour market conditions. At the same time as FUTURES was introduced an economic recovery began to reduce the youth unemployment rate (see Table 1 on p. 29). By 1989 the youth unemployment rate had decreased to less than half of its 1983 level. Ironically for MSD, the decrease in the youth unemployment rate represented, at best, a dubious outcome. In its first year of operation the FUTURES program underspent its $129 million budget by $17 million. Youth programs budgets continued to be chronically underspent from 1986 to 1990, accounting for the majority of the underspending of the ministry. The underspending of MSD is shown in Table 4 and compared to the spending patterns of other ministries. The table demonstrates that during each year of MSD's existence it underspent its budget and that the underspending increased from 1986 to 1988. In 1988 the underspending accounted for 15 percent of the ministry's total budget. In 1986, 1987, and 1988 MSD had a larger negative variance (unspent budget at the end of the year) in both real and percentage terms than other ministries and MSD was the only ministry to have a negative variance for all five years. The implications of the chronic underspending are discussed later in this chapter and in the next.

**Table 4: Variance Between Budgeted and Actual Expenditures for Selected Ministries, 1986 to 1990 (millions of dollars)**

| Year | MCU | MCSS | Ministry MoEd | MITT | MoL | MSD |
|---|---|---|---|---|---|---|
| 1986 | | | | | | |
| Budget | 2,053 | 2,768 | 3,385 | 82 | 75 | 418 |
| Actual | 2,063 | 2,863 | 3,380 | 82 | 76 | 392 |
| Variance | +10 | +95 | -5 | 0 | +1 | -26 |
| 1987 | | | | | | |
| Budget | 2,128 | 3,133 | 3,585 | 176 | 92 | 459 |
| Actual | 2,254 | 3,285 | 3,937 | 197 | 97 | 405 |
| Variance | +126 | +152 | +352 | +30 | +5 | -54 |
| 1988 | | | | | | |
| Budget | 2,400 | 3,636 | 4,382 | 174 | 111 | 455 |
| Actual | 2,391 | 3,775 | 4,447 | 173 | 107 | 385 |
| Variance | -9 | +139 | +65 | -1 | -4 | -70 |
| 1989 | | | | | | |
| Budget | 2,583 | 4,308 | 4,799 | 171 | 126 | 408 |
| Actual | 2,668 | 4,312 | 5,111 | 156 | 119 | 402 |
| Variance | +85 | +4 | +312 | -15 | -7 | -6 |
| 1990 | | | | | | |
| Budget | 2,746 | 5,056 | 5,210 | 268 | 139 | 433 |
| Actual | 2,731 | 5,062 | 5,321 | 156 | 119 | 415 |
| Variance | -15 | +6 | +111 | -60 | -6 | -18 |

Key: Budget = budgeted expenditures for the year.
     Actual = actual expenditures for the year.
     Variance = variance (actual less budget).

     MCU = Ministry of Colleges and Universities
     MCSS = Ministry of Community and Social Services
     MoEd = Ministry of Education
     MITT = Ministry of Industry, Trade and Technology
     MoL = Ministry of Labour
     MSD = Ministry of Skills Development

Note: The budgets are for fiscal years. For example, 1986 refers to 1 April 1986 to 31 March 1987.

Source: Ministry of Treasury and Economics, *Public Accounts*. Annual.

## LEADERSHIP

The ability of the new ministry to quickly introduce FUTURES and the training strategy was due, in part, to the nature of its leadership. In going to Cabinet, MSD and MCU shared the same minister who was able to act, in his own words, as "the final arbitrator" between his two ministries. With respect to the training strategy, Sorbara recalls that "at the last moment MCU staff raised serious questions about the proposal, and the role of the colleges. I was about to remove the item from the Cabinet agenda, but was able to successfully resolve the issues between the ministries and later proceed to Cabinet." The resolution of the issues, in his view, would have proven more difficult, if not impossible, had both ministries not shared the same minister.

For MSD, a joint minister had positive and negative effects. On the positive side, a joint minister meant that MCU could not ignore MSD and its concerns. On the negative side, training policy garnered less time and interest, if only because the minister had less time available. The postsecondary institutions were demanding in their desire to have direct access to the minister, while the skills training ministry's stakeholders were far less organized and challenging. Furthermore, the total spending by the colleges and university ministry was five times that of the training agency's. Finally, a joint minister meant that the training ministry could never quite be certain that its own minister was acting just on its behalf.

Decisions by MSD's leaders in developing the training strategy in 1986 began a pattern that was to have detrimental effects for the organization. One central agency official explained that, "the strategy was flawed because MSD developed it without consultation with other ministries," especially since colleges were to be a prime delivery agent of the programs in the strategy. The Cabinet submission for the initiative makes no mention of consultation with other ministries and fails to analyze the impact of the initiative on other ministries.

Although interministry cooperation is often an elusive objective, it is significant that MSD's leaders did not even bother to go through the motions to consult other ministries. One Cabinet member expressed the view that "the overall problem for MSD in those early years, was a sense that it was involved in too much research and glitzy advocacy and not enough of what some people felt was its real mandate, namely to change attitudes and programs in ministries like Education and Labour and the powerful constituencies which those departments represented, both within and outside of government" (correspondence with the author).

One explanation for lack of interministry consultation on the strategy is the newness of MSD. The administrative leadership of the training ministry, especially in the policy division, was new to a line-ministry environment. There was also no corporate history and culture at the ministry on how to interact with other ministries and central agencies. The reflection of an MSD assistant deputy minister in 1989 on this matter (in a report to his superiors on the future of the ministry) provides additional evidence for a miscalculation on the part of the MSD in dealing with others. The official wrote that: "in building the organization and developing new programs, we have not paid enough time [sic] to *horizontal consensus-building in government*" (emphasis in original). The document goes on to add that "as the rationale for our existence was itself an affront to those who lost certain of their activities, we have operated in an environment of controversy and acted with zeal and energy to demonstrate our usefulness. This has caused problems." One effect of MSD's zeal was the reputation that it acquired with central agency staff and other ministries.

MSD was described by others in government as "arrogant," "aggressive," "not willing to listen," "difficult," and "negative." The descriptions must, to some extent, be viewed as referring to the leaders of MSD and their personalities. This view of MSD was not restricted to MCU (where one might logically expect it) but was widespread in other ministries. Central agency staff believed that MSD "needed to be pushed to consult and to do things with more collegiality"; "was not being a team player"; "had a street fighting approach"; and "adopted a non-consultative approach .... which was not helpful." Cabinet ministers, perhaps trying to more diplomatically express similar views, called MSD staff "extremely committed and dedicated" and "setting ambitious goals." The MSD staff described themselves and their corporate culture as "more 'entrepreneurial,' 'innovative' and 'flexible' [in] character than that of the [other] ministries" (McFadyen 1994, p. 136).

An illustration of the MSD's *modus operandi* was the release of a report in mid-1987 on industrial training for women. In a sharp reprimand from the secretary of Cabinet, copied to the premier's office, the MSD deputy was told:

> As was previously discussed, I am concerned about your lack of consultation ... on the Training for Women in the Workplace study. I was, however, unaware at the time when we spoke about this issue that the study involved a public opinion poll or marketing study. Your ministry did not furnish adequate time to ... the Office of the Premier for the tabling of this material and permit others to review it and take the necessary steps for its proper release.
>
> On this or any other sensitive issue, I would expect that more attention would be given to providing adequate time and attention to the concerns of other ministries and the role Cabinet Office ... It is unacceptable when such reports are received the afternoon before they are to be released (H. Ezrin collection, Archives of Ontario).

Not only were MSD's leaders inexperienced in consulting others, they also believed that they needed to be assertive (if not aggressive) if policy changes were to be made. They feared being co-opted by the institutional interests of the education ministries and the social policy demands of other agencies. However, the isolationist course would ultimately come to serve MSD poorly.

## DIVISION FROM WITHIN

A second area in which the ministry's leaders made strategic errors was in guiding the development of a corporate culture. Given their differing functions it is not uncommon for the policy and operations divisions of a line ministry to experience a degree of friction. In MSD's case, the situation became dysfunctional and was widely discussed in the public service inducing one MSD deputy minister to refer to it as "the ministry's terrible problem." Individuals in the operations division referred to the policy division as "enemies" and "the ivory tower." Operations staff viewed the policy division as unnecessarily garnering new resources and staff, which were not used to serve clients in the "real" world. Staff in both divisions characterized the relationship between the divisions by using words such as "an incredible gulf" and "two solitudes." A deputy minister of MSD noted that "the lack of internal cohesion meant that the ministry could not deal with external threats ... which made the ministry an easy prey." The deputy went on to add that "internally the ministry did not work."

The causes of this gulf were six-fold. First, the operations division was an amalgamation of formerly separate units not used to working with a strong centre dictating policy. Second, the policy division was created in 1985 while many of the units of the operations division, such as the apprenticeship branch, had histories and organizational cultures that had developed over decades. Third, the policy division was primarily composed of individuals with backgrounds in economics and political science who saw their client as the minister and Cabinet, while the training division was comprised of program managers and deliverers who saw their client as the trainee and employer. As noted above, differing views between policy and operations officials are not restricted to the MSD, but because it was a new organization a common value system had yet to be forged through the normal course of events, nor had specific mechanisms been instituted to act as catalysts. What was unique and dysfunctional is that neither group thought that its expertise and knowledge was valuable to the other. Indeed, there was very little mobility of staff from one division to the other, notwithstanding that nearly all the ministry's staff were located in downtown Toronto.

Fourth, the two divisions were located in different buildings in Toronto, so that there was little opportunity for informal contact between the respective staff. The spatial separation reinforced the gulf between the two divisions by excluding the possibility of informal interaction between members of the two groups in washrooms, elevators, and hallways. The inability to interact meant that stereotypes became reinforced, with operations staff coming to believe that the policy group was making mistakes and dealing only with packaging rather than the substantive issues. On the other hand, the policy group saw the operations division as unable to take new policy directions and implement new programs giving rise to underspending such as with the FUTURES program.

Fifth, MSD's initial leadership (minister and deputy minister) was insufficiently attuned to the need to forge a coherent and cohesive organizational culture. Sorbara, like all ministers in the new government, was inexperienced in his new role. Tully was a "policy deputy" who assumed that policy drives a new ministry and had little interest (or background) in organizational dynamics. In any case, the more immediate pressures on the leadership were to formalize the organizational structure and consolidate programs, rather than to tend to internal dynamics.

Sixth, the assistant deputy ministers of the two divisions did not get along. The conflict between the individuals (known as the "warring assistant deputies") was both a cause and a reflection of the lack of cohesiveness of the ministry. It was a reflection of the disparate "world views" of each division. At the same time the tension between the divisional leaders reinforced the friction and hostility between the two camps. The conflict apparently was based on different views of issues (such as whether MSD was primarily a social or economic policy ministry), as well as differences in personality.

The two corporate subcultures which emerged meant that strategic directions for the organization as a whole were precarious at best. The shared corporate values and norms that did exist among senior staff were entrepreneurship and innovation. By their very nature these values did not breed a cohesive view of what MSD should be. The internal schism gave the appearance to others in government of a dysfunctional organization at odds with itself. Observers outside the provincial government had also become aware of the internal problems at MSD. A federal official discerned that "there was a split between the policy and delivery divisions of the ministry. Both divisions seemed to work in isolation from each other. For apprenticeship, the ministry argued against private-sector [in classroom] training, but in the field the operations division allowed private-sector training as a part of apprenticeship."

In addition to the split within the skills development ministry, some staff continued to harbour loyalties to their "home" ministries, rather than MSD. The problem existed because it took several years for all skills development staff to be consolidated in one location. For two or three years MSD operations staff and MCU staff were working side by side (as was the case prior to 1985) although they were members of different ministries. The problem of divided loyalties was compounded by the resentment of operations staff toward the policy group. As such, some units at MSD constituted potentially subversive elements within the organization and, at the very least, likely were important sources of intelligence for other ministries.

Beginning in 1988 MSD's leadership began a strategic planning exercise to address the dysfunctional corporate culture. The strategic plan completed in 1989 stated that "the ministry will move the planning and implementation functions closer together" (MSD 1989c, p.7). However, as will be seen in the next chapter, by that time the ministry had squandered control over its future.

## CONCLUSION

In reviewing MSD's birth, it is evident that the organization was created to address three sets of interrelated, yet conceptually distinct, problems: political, administrative, and policy. Politically, a new ministry enabled the novice Miller government to present itself as different from the Davis regime, and proactive in its approach to social and economic issues. Furthermore, it allowed the government to be seen as dealing with youth unemployment and labour market matters.

The second cause for MSD's creation was administrative. The new ministry centralized many of the fragmented government responsibilities for youth and training (hopefully) to increase effectiveness and efficiency. The timing of the establishment of the ministry was also related to the need for the province to react in a more coordinated and centralized manner to federal government policy shifts in labour market policy. Moreover, the new ministry provided an organizational (rather than policy) solution as to which ministry should have responsibility for coordinating labour market adjustment policy.

The third reason for MSD's establishment was dissatisfaction with existing programs that placed insufficient importance on active labour market policy. Labour market adjustment was becoming an important issue and there was increasing concern, fostered by the manpower commission, about the inadequate skill level of Ontario's labour force, and the role of government in bringing about change. There was little agreement by policymakers in the mid-1980s about what policy changes were required, beyond the immediate need to react to federal government policy changes. A new organization provided a mechanism for new policies to emerge.

The three sets of reasons for the creation of MSD were not mutually exclusive. In fact, the opposite was the case. For example, the high rate of youth unemployment was a political, administrative, and policy problem. Similarly, the actions of the federal government called for political, administrative, and policy responses. The skills development ministry came into existence precisely because the three sets of problems or conditions overlapped and could be addressed with one solution. Each of the three problems, on its own, would have been incapable of eliciting a new organization.

The relatively low level of scrutiny by Cabinet and other central agencies during the early years, caused by disinterest and other priorities, meant that MSD went largely unnoticed by the centre. This allowed the ministry's administrative leadership to be aggressive in staking out a domain for the organization and introducing new programs, or at least repackaging existing ones. The joint minister with the colleges and universities ministry caused training ministry staff to believe that their ministry always had an ally at the Cabinet table.

The emergence of the new ministry caused competitive pressures regarding domain to arise between it and MCU. This is not surprising since organizations "that provide similar outputs ... may regard each other as threatening or as constraining their individual efforts to offer a comprehensive response to a problem or need" (Molnar and Rogers 1979, p. 410). Some of this competition (such as between industrial and institutional training) existed before the arrival of MSD, but its focus changed with the introduction of the organizational structure, the increasing emphasis on industrial training, and the new political regime.

The decrease in youth unemployment levels caused MSD to continually underspend its budget, and initiated questions about the performance of the ministry. Underspending implied that either MSD's policies and programs were inappropriate for the labour market conditions or that the programs were poorly implemented and administered. That other ministries, especially the education ones, regularly overspent budgets suggested to many in Cabinet that the objectives being pursued by other ministries were more urgent than MSD's.

The ministry's leadership chose to act in an aggressive or competitive manner. Part of the aggressiveness was due to the turmoil characterizing the time of its birth, necessitating aggressive tactics to survive and flourish. In other words, actions of the ministry's leaders reflected the times and conditions in which it was born. The regulation of interministry relations was left largely to the joint minister between MSD and MCU. A second reason for MSD's combativeness is that given the precarious values and fragmented jurisdiction inherent in the policy field, there was no choice but to act aggressively. Without a strong policy capacity and leaders willing to battle the preconceived notions and interests of other ministries, the MSD would never coordinate policy. In other words, to make training a less precarious value, both within the political sphere and in the larger society, the ministry's leaders felt that bold actions were required to battle the entrenched interests, especially those of educational institutions.

A cohesive internal culture failed to materialize at the new ministry, in part because early leaders gave insufficient attention to corporate culture. Conflicts between the policy and operations groups made program implementation difficult, precipitating incongruence between policy and program delivery.

Notwithstanding an unclear mandate, domain overlap, changing economic conditions, and internal instability, the new organization not only survived, but also gained approval for new initiatives. What explains MSD's early success? Three conditions were key in allowing the organization to operate relatively effectively from 1985 to 1987: leaders who saw MSD's mandate in economic policy, a shared leader with MCU, and newness.

The decision by Tully and Horswill in 1985 that MSD had an economic, rather than social, policy mandate helped to draw boundaries around the ministry's domain. These would later be amplified, but initially they served the ministry well by imposing some certainty about its domain. The shared minister with MCU provided MSD, if not always with an ally, at least with a known quantity at Cabinet, especially when dealing with the colleges. The young age of MSD meant that errors, such as underspending on youth programs, could be explained as representing the normal learning curve. Two years were insufficient to allow a determination about whether the organization was successful in shifting labour market adjustment policy toward decreased fragmentation and overlap, more coordination and a less precarious state.

The challenge for the ministry by mid-1987 was three-fold: first, to continue developing and coordinating policy, while rationalizing programs in an arena in which previous organizational arrangements had proven unsatisfactory; second, to successfully manage relationships with older and established ministries that had a stake and role in training policy; and finally, to construct a strong and cohesive corporate culture that would allow the organization to effectively pursue government objectives.

# 3

# The Fall of the Ministry of Skills Development: Unable to Deliver

*The long ... years of ... middle-aged adversity are*
*excellent campaigning weather for the Devil.*
Clive Staples Lewis (1898-1963)

The mid-1987 provincial election provided the Liberals with a majority government leading to a lessening of political upheaval. Freed of its obligations under the minority government, Peterson began developing his own agenda emphasizing Ontario's competitive position in the global economy. A priority of the government became "to modernize [the] training system and ensure that Ontario's workforce has the skills and flexibility to adjust to changing technological requirements" (Speech from the Throne, *Hansard*, Legislative Assembly of Ontario, No. 3, 1987, p. 6). Moreover, the Canada-US Free Trade Agreement heightened the urgency for an active labour market policy in support of the province's economic position.

## HIGH EXPECTATIONS AND FRUSTRATIONS

In fall 1987, the Ministry of Skills Development (MSD) was given its own minister, Alving Curling, and a new deputy minister, Glenna Carr. The same day that Curling was appointed minister, the premier announced that the community-based literacy programs from the Ministry of Citizenship would be transferred to MSD. A senior official at the citizenship ministry recalled: "I woke up one morning to find that literacy programs had been moved to MSD without consulting the minister or deputy of Citizenship."

The surprising transfer of literacy policy to the skills development ministry was explicitly designed to mollify Curling who had publicly expressed his desire to remain in his previous portfolio as housing minister. Curling had a well-known commitment to literacy and the transfer of this function was designed to sweeten his appointment to MSD and increase the clout of the ministry. Nevertheless, his move from housing to the training ministry was widely perceived as a significant demotion since as skills development minister he would possess less influence than at the housing portfolio.

The transfer of the literacy funding to the skills development ministry to appease Curling did little to make the portfolio less junior. It did, however, illustrate that training remained a precarious field in which shifts in domain occurred at the whim of the first minister with little, if any, planning or policy rationale. Funding for community or non-school literacy ($5 million per year) comprised only a small component of the total literacy programs in Ontario, the majority of which were provided by school boards. Moreover, MSD's involvement in adult literacy policy was a departure for a ministry that had been focused on industrial training and youth employment for the past two years. The literacy programs became the fifth and final program cluster — in addition to youth, industrial/pre-employment, apprenticeship, and programs for laid-off workers — in the ministry's portfolio.

Having responsibility for literacy programs caused domain overlap to crop up with the Ministry of Education (MoEd) which funded literacy programs via school boards. The education ministry had expressed a desire to acquire the community (non-school board) literacy programs since it already possessed prime responsibility for ensuring literacy through its institutions. Senior education ministry officials believed, as one stated, that "community literacy made more sense to be in Education." On the other hand, MSD officials, as one stated, "perceived the education ministry to be the last place to position literacy since that ministry had failed illiterate adults when they were children ... Furthermore, Education with its strong institutional links was not likely to support independent community organizations." A split between institutional literacy programs (delivered via school boards) and non-institutional literacy programs (delivered via community-based groups) was developing, similar to the industrial-institutional split in labour market training.

To the optimists, late 1987 was the high point of MSD's influence and prestige. It no longer had a shared or part-time minister, but now had a full-time one who could devote his full energies to the department. Furthermore, its mission had been expanded by the premier to encompass literacy policy, signifying that its work in the previous two years was bearing fruit. Finally, it had acquired additional resources and responsibility to implement two new initiatives (the Transitions program and the Help Centres) for laid-off workers. These circumstances suggested that the initial uncertainty and lack of legitimacy of the organization might now be on the verge of being overcome. A paradox of the ministry's history is that the apparently cheerful situation at the end of 1987 masked the grave crises that were to threaten the organization.

By late 1987 it was apparent that the combination of Curling's interests and those of his deputy, along with the transfer of literacy policy, had propelled the ministry away from primarily supporting economic development. Both Curling and Carr had social policy backgrounds and veered MSD to meet the needs of the disadvantaged in society. For example, Carr had spend her 15-year career in the Ontario public service in a series of positions dealing with affirmative action and women's issues. The shift and expansion of mandate reinforced the view, held by some at Queen's Park, that the ministry's objectives and domain were ill-defined.

A strategic planning process was begun in 1988 by Curling and Carr, the first effort since Bill 9 in 1985 to define the ministry's mission. The outcome of the planning process, which was essentially a consultation with ministry staff about what should be the agency's objectives, were six organizational goals: creating a training culture in Ontario, eliminating illiteracy, increasing the skill level of workers, encouraging a greater federal role, studying labour market trends, and assisting social assistance recipients to become employed. These differ significantly from those of Bill 9, especially the addition of the goals to eliminate illiteracy and assist social assistance recipients. MSD, clearly, had migrated into the social policy arena.

Illustrative of the ministry's performance after 1987 was the proposal to expand apprenticeship. The expansion had been approved in principle by Cabinet in mid-1987 and announced during the election campaign. In 1988, the ministry returned to Cabinet to state (in a document that was eventually leaked to the press) that:

> On August 21, 1987 Cabinet approved a series of initiatives designed to strengthen and modernize the apprenticeship system. These were announced by the Premier on August 31, 1987. The Ministry of Skills Development has not been allocated the resources originally requested to implement the initiatives. The Ministry wishes to inform Cabinet of the implications of that decision ... The apprenticeship initiatives were developed to address a number of pressing economic and social concerns. Chief among these was the need to provide Ontario firms with the skilled tradespeople they need to remain competitive. They are sought to improve vocational training opportunities for women and youth. The original submission approved by Cabinet requested $14.6 million in new expenditures. This would have included creation of 54 new positions needed to implement the initiatives. Bearing in mind the Treasurer's message of fiscal restraint, the Ministry reduced its request to 39 new positions in 1988/89, the minimum increase needed to give effect to Cabinet's decision. While Management Board staff originally acknowledged the need for such increases, the Ministry has not been provided with the resources needed to implement the initiatives.

The failure of the ministry to obtain the resources can be interpreted in different ways. The proposal could have been poor and approved only in principle to be used as part of the election campaign. Or Curling might have lacked the skills to convince his Cabinet colleagues of the importance of the proposal and build the necessary coalition to ensure its acceptance. Alternatively, the chronic underspending of the ministry might have made Cabinet hesitant to allocate additional resources. And finally, the proposal could have floundered because it did not build on a larger vision — supported by business and labour stakeholders — of the role of apprenticeship.

The failure to garner Cabinet approval was, as suggested above, the result of a combination of causes. Prime among these was the underestimation by the minister and novice deputy of the degree of coalition-building required, especially in light of the persistent pattern of underspending on new initiatives. In other words, the leadership failed to realize how precarious the ministry's position had come to be. The inability of the ministry to obtain additional funds for the only program that it directly delivered is an important event in its history. Under its own minister it failed to gain assent for an initiative — already approved in principle — at a time when the government as a whole was placing increased importance on labour market policy.

In early 1988, the Policy and Priorities Board of Cabinet instructed MSD to head up the development of a comprehensive labour market strategy for the government. This request, in response to the increase in global competition and increasing layoffs in the manufacturing sector, seemed to vindicate the ministry's efforts to raise the profile of labour market adjustment policies and confirm the ministry's leadership role. In drafting the paper for Cabinet one MSD participant recalled "long and heated discussions between senior staff at Skills [at the director and assistant deputy minister level] and staff at other ministries over particular words to be used in the paper." The final product failed to reflect the interests and concerns of various stakeholders — business, labour, and the education/training institutions — and was summarily dismissed by Cabinet.

The failed policy paper, combined with the inability to reform apprenticeship, and continual underspending raised questions about MSD's performance and its ability to meet government objectives. Central agency staff began to believe that the ministry's future was uncertain, and increasingly so as time went on. According to one Cabinet Office official, by mid-1988, "there were more and more discussions as to when Skills Development would disappear."

The ministry's performance and low degree of legitimacy are reflected in comments made by members of Opposition parties in the Legislature, such as those by the NDP critic for MSD:

In 10 years as a member I have a number of times called for the resignation of a minister, but this is the first time that I have asked a government to seriously consider getting rid of a ministry in its entirety. It seems to me that the time to make the decision to scrap the Ministry of Skills Development is at hand for a number of reasons.

It is a clearly incoherent ministry which does not know what it is doing ... A number of its functions would much better be handled under other line ministries, like the Ministry of Labour and the Ministry of Education for literacy. There is really no need for this ministry to continue, unless the government just wants to spend money on extra public relations, for a minister to be able to go around and make certain announcements that could be made by other ministries. I have to tell members that it again has underspent its money this year for some of those disadvantaged people of our society who need help (*Hansard*, 12 December 1988, p. 6659).

The Progressive Conservative Party was not enamoured by MSD, notwithstanding that it had created the organization a few years earlier, as explained by the Conservative critic for MSD:

In 1986-87, underspending by the ministry was $55 million and last year underspending was a whopping $77 million. For the last two years, budgetary allocation for the ministry decreased by $1 million last year and then was slashed by a further $47 million this year.

This tells me two things. First, the programs are not working. What little spending there is is clearly directed towards advertising and publications ... Second, this shows me that the government is not interested in correcting the problems of mismanagement and lack of planning. We really wish the Treasurer would do so, especially in this ministry (*Hansard*, 26 April 1988, p. 2782).

In July 1989, Michael Harris, the Conservative House Leader (who would in 1990 become party leader) weighed in with:

I really question the Treasurer and the Chairman of the Management Board of Cabinet allowing this hodgepodge, the myriad of programs. The minister himself calls it an "array of programs", none of which has worked so far, wasting millions and millions and millions of dollars, as a number of my colleagues in both parties on this side of the House have pointed out ... It is apparent from talking to people in the field all over this province that it is a total and unmitigated disaster: the minister, the whole ministry and all of the programs (*Hansard*, 11 July 1989, p. 2069).

The comments by both Opposition parties, in 1988 and 1989, made it obvious to the Liberals that there would be little outcry in the Legislature, or the broader community, if the organization were to disappear.

The views of the MSD held by the Opposition, central agencies, and line ministries, had serious consequences for the ministry's staff. As expressed by one Cabinet member, by early 1989 MSD was "experiencing an 'existential crisis' brought about by its continual quest for legitimacy." A central agency official believed that over time "the people at MSD became shell shocked and dysfunctional because of the cloud of uncertainty. Skills Development spent energy just trying to stay alive."

The ministry's last gasp came in 1989 when it obtained approval for three initiatives budgeted at $6.6 million annually. The three programs illustrate increasing fragmentation and ad hoc policy. The traineeship program was a shorter, more flexible version of the formal apprenticeship model, for industrial sectors (such as hospitality) which did not have apprenticeships. The second program, the school workplace apprenticeship program, allowed high school students to begin apprenticeship training while in high school. The third program provided a wage subsidy to employers who hired summer students as apprentices. These programs, expected to serve only 1,900 clients in the first year of operation and 2,900 in the second year of operation, were at odds with the grandiose title of the Cabinet submission that sought their approval: "Proposal to Introduce Programs to Equip Workers for the Skill Demands of the 1990s." In any case, the introduction of additional programs for youth was peculiar at a time when youth unemployment was low, while the growth in the number of small programs was a perverse development for an organization created to consolidate and better coordinate disparate programs.

Key decisionmakers came to believe that after FUTURES and the training strategy in 1986, MSD began to falter in its performance. Peterson expressed the opinion that "MSD worked reasonably well at the beginning" especially in tackling youth unemployment, but less so later. With respect to the training area he thought that "the organizational structure was never right" and that there was need to "play with structures to get things a little better." A member of Cabinet stated that there was "a sense of frustration at the lack of performance and coordination in training and education ... and at the fact that key players in the Ontario government were not well coordinated with respect to training ... We were spending a lot of money and time, but there did not seem to be a focus."

Only a handful of senior policymakers outside MSD understood that some of the dilemmas facing the ministry were inherent in the policy field. One noted the "vague and amorphous nature of training" and the simplistic view held by colleagues in central agencies of possible solutions. Another stated that although there was displeasure at the skills development ministry, "few in key positions realized that the ministry grew out of a history of failed policy and programming in manpower planning in which no single ministry or group of ministries had previously succeeded."

## LEADERSHIP

One reason for the dissatisfaction by the centre with MSD's performance was the ministry's leadership during this time. Curling had no vision of labour market adjustment policy other than the importance of literacy, a theme that tended to take centre-stage in his speeches. At times he seemed to justify MSD's existence solely on the illiteracy rate in the province. In answer to a question from the Opposition as to why his ministry was needed, Curling said: "We need a ministry committed to training because when we saw the illiteracy rate and the kind of skills that people had in Ontario, 24 per cent of adults were functionally illiterate" (*Hansard*, 22 November 1988, p. 6035).

Curling did not possess the personal status and influence to, as one Cabinet Office official stated, "hold the attention of Cabinet or the Premier" and build coalitions. In hindsight, Curling came to believe that his Cabinet colleagues "did not fully understand the challenges of the ministry" and were "waiting for me to be more aggressive" in advocating for training. Looking back, he added that he "should have been more aggressive in explaining to colleagues ... especially those with the money." Curling's performance was not a result of being poorly briefed by his ministry or somehow sabotaged by his staff, nor was it the case that Curling appeared to be uninterested in his portfolio or failed to work hard on behalf of MSD.

The negative opinion of key actors about Curling's performance might represent an after-the-fact rationalization for the eventual failure of the ministry. Partly, Curling was believed to be a poor leader since his demotion from housing to MSD hinted that his career was in decline. His emphasis on literacy policy heightened uncertainty, on the part of others, about MSD's core mission while being at odds with Cabinet's desire for training to be intimately linked to economic policy. Also, Curling had less clout as a leader than Sorbara because he did not have oversight of the colleges and universities ministry.

The fact that Curling was black might have caused some to speculate that his position in Cabinet was due not to expertise but to ensure the representation of minorities. This initially would have created an expectation (which became self-fulfilling) that he was a weak leader. Another explanation is that others had placed extraordinarily high expectations on Curling because he was black, which were unattainable. Finally, it could be the case that a black leader of a powerful ministry, such as housing, will prove successful, but that a black leader of a more junior ministry will be dismissed as a token appointment.

It is simplistic to attribute MSD's inadequate performance after 1987 to Curling alone. While poor and inappropriate political leadership played an important role in the manner that developments occurred, the eventual outcome was not due solely, or even primarily, to Curling. While minister of housing from 1985 to 1987 Curling had expanded that department's influence and staff, gaining a measure of respect for dealing with rent control legislation. At the same time, it is also clear that Curling's expertise was not suited to providing effective leadership for MSD. His strength as a leader, as he himself acknowledged, was in acting as a conciliator and mediator: a role he fulfilled well at the housing ministry vis-à-vis tenants and landlords. Indeed, Curling's leadership skills were suited to an organization with institutionalized and sophisticated stakeholders holding well-developed ideological positions requiring a minister with strong interpersonal skills who could assist them to find common ground. At MSD he found himself the leader of a ministry with few constituents that required him not to mediate but to create and advocate policies in an environment of precarious values. He described the skills development ministry as very different from his previous portfolio because he felt no evidence of "strong emotions, as had been the case at Housing."

The deputy minister, Carr, failed to replace the feuding assistant deputy ministers: a decision that if taken would have had immediate benefits for the organization. Although there is nothing to suggest that Carr was not a capable deputy, the fact that she was a novice in the position made her more hesitant than required by events and conditions. For example, the strategic planning exercise she instituted came too late. A more forceful deputy, with greater clout, could have counteracted, or at least minimized, Curling's weaknesses while placing more stress on working cooperatively with other agencies.

The MSD staff felt that obtaining a full-time minister in 1987 was a sign of the worth that the government now placed on training policy and bolstered their department's position vis-à-vis other ministries. Ironically, and unbeknownst to many participants and observers at the time, MSD took a crucial step toward decline when it gained its own minister because it lost whatever support and linkages it might have had to the colleges and universities ministry at the Cabinet table.

## IMPROVING COORDINATION

During 1985-87 there were no formal mechanisms — other than the shared MSD-MCU minister — to coordinate labour market adjustment policies. In early 1987 the deputy ministers of skills development, MCU, and MoEd established a committee of senior staff to provide "a forum for issue and policy coordination, and for joint policy and program development among the three ministries" (internal report, 1988). The committee was chaired, on a rotating basis, by assistant deputy ministers from the three ministries.

The committee was the first, and most rudimentary, formal attempt to coordinate labour market adjustment policy, though the forum dealt only with non-contentious issues on which agreement could easily be reached, such as the research priorities each ministry would pursue. For example, from mid-1987 to mid-1988 the group appraised the effectiveness of career counselling in the school-to-work transition. The provision of labour market information transpired within the institutions and programs of the three ministries, therefore representing a common interest. The committee's report concluded that career counselling was important, that additional research was required, and that each ministry had a number of separate initiatives underway to address related issues without considering how the resources of the three ministries could be reallocated to improve the fragmented information services. By stating the obvious and not presenting new directions, the report (not surprisingly) met with indifference from the three deputies. On this and other matters, the committee failed to coordinate policies because its members did not have the power or incentive to deal with contentious or strategic issues. Furthermore, the committee was not a priority among the deputies because their ministers faced different pressures.

An outcome of the failed 1988 strategic labour market policy paper developed by MSD for Cabinet was the creation by Cabinet of a five-ministry forum — MSD, MCU, MoEd, MoL, and the industry ministry — to develop a labour market strategy for the province. The new forum was a recognition by central agencies that it was impossible to design labour market policies inside one ministry, and that the tri-ministry committee was ineffective. Most participants recalled that the industry ministry was the lead agency; however, some people felt that it was the skills development ministry. This, in itself, is evidence of the lack of direction from the centre for this exercise and, indeed, for labour market policy in general. That (apparently) the industry ministry, and not the training ministry, was given the lead by Cabinet for policy development clearly was a sign of dissatisfaction by central agencies of MSD's ability to work with other ministries.

The five-ministry group prepared a strategic policy paper, which received approval in principle from Cabinet in February 1989. The secretary of the Cabinet's policy and priorities board in writing to the five deputy ministers noted that:

> The next steps in the process, of course, present a real challenge to all of us. As you know from the meeting, both the Premier and the Treasurer support the need to address labour market issues ... However, I note their concerns about ensuring that we get the package of labour market program enhancements and proposals "right" the first time through. I also note the concerns of the Board about the importance of ensuring the effectiveness and efficiency of the proposed package, the need to minimize duplication, the need to review existing programs to determine where resources might be reallocated to higher priorities.

The paper allowed the five ministries to continue to develop proposals in 13 areas: incentives for training by industry, cooperative education, centres of specialization in postsecondary institutions, regulatory reform, and so forth. A coherent strategy was to emerge, as asserted in the paper, from the specific proposals based on "the themes of building partnerships with the private sector and institutions, sharing information and ensuring a supportive environment." Each ministry viewed the interministry group as an opportunity to obtain additional resources for its own programs and projects, making little effort to tackle issues in an integrated or strategic manner or to review existing policies. In the end, no specific proposals were ever considered by Cabinet, notwithstanding the efforts of staff at the various ministries and Cabinet Office.

This moved Cabinet to expand the forum to include the social policy ministries — social services and citizenship — with linkages to labour market policy. The hope was that the addition of social policy perspectives on labour market matters would cause ministries to cooperate on a more strategic level. The two ministries had been critical of previous policy efforts because they felt these ignored social policy problems, such as (re)entry into the labour market of persons on social assistance, the disabled, and immigrants. However, history repeated itself. The expanded committee was unwieldy and simply created seven shopping lists, rather than five, and was no more successful than its predecessor.

The failures at interministry policy development finally made it clear to Peterson that there were severe difficulties in getting ministries to work together to craft creative and integrated proposals. To engender more coordination between ministries, and to impose a higher degree of regulation from the centre, Sean Conway was made minister of MSD, MCU, and MoEd in August 1989, responsible for all education and training policy. Conway, because of his stature (he had previously been government House Leader while also holding ministerial portfolios), political acumen, and long-standing commitment to the provincial Liberal Party was a very powerful, important minister.

A joint minister for the three ministries addressed one of the problems of interministry cooperation, namely that there is little in it for the ministers, since the very notion of ministerial responsibility makes interministerial undertakings difficult. Ministers bear the ultimate burden for the performance of the department they head and may have to resign if shortcomings arise within their portfolios or they could be shuffled by the first minister to the back benches. In such an environment there is only miniscule incentive for collaboration since successful collaboration brings little benefit to any single minister, while increasing the likelihood that any failures will spread to infect more than one minister.

At the same time as Conway was made "super minister" of education and training, the premier established a new Cabinet committee on education, training, and adjustment chaired by Conway which was charged with "the development of a labour market strategy for the 1990's" (Premier's Office 1989*a*). The Cabinet committee brought Cabinet ministers into active roles vis-à-vis labour market adjustment policy. This new committee was part of a larger realignment of Cabinet committees designed to allow policymakers to better focus on priorities and ensure streamlined decision making.

A month after Conway's appointment and the creation of the Cabinet committee, Peterson announced that the deputy minister of MoEd, Bernard Shapiro, would also serve as acting deputy minister of MSD while continuing as deputy minister of education. Shapiro's mandate, as outlined by the premier, was to oversee "organizational changes ... designed to integrate education, training and labour adjustment" (Premier's Office 1989*b*). The appointments of Conway and Shapiro are evidence that Peterson was now less convinced that effective policy would arise through a competitive process and that a more top-down approach was unavoidable.

The mid-1989 changes in government structures — a new Cabinet committee, a joint minister, and a shared deputy minister — improved coordination to some degree. In February 1990 a discussion paper proposing a new direction for labour market adjustment policy was discussed by the new Cabinet committee. The theme of the paper was that novel arrangements were required based on a more equitable sharing of responsibility among government and the other labour market "partners." However, the appendix of the paper listed, by ministry, 130 new proposals and program expansions spread among eight ministries demonstrating that ministries were still presenting shopping lists, rather than reviewing existing policies and programs to determine how to better allocate resources. According to a senior Cabinet Office official "none of the efforts, including the Cabinet committee, was truly successful in overcoming the interministry rivalry."

The inability of the government to make progress in addressing training issues resulted in yet another structural response. In 1989, the Premier's Council was asked by Peterson to "work on its new agenda — an in-depth study of education, training and labour adjustment issues" (Premier's Council 1989*b*, p. 1). Established in 1986, the Council was composed of the premier, several ministers, and leaders of the business, labour, and academic communities. The Council operated independently of the public service, reporting not to a ministry but directly to the premier. The composition of the Premier's Council, and the fact that the premier was its chair, gave it more prestige and influence than other external advisory groups.

The discussions at the Premier's Council provided a forum for those inside and outside government who were critical of the skills development ministry. One member of the Council said that in meetings he "argued that the skills ministry be done away with because the ministry could not win battles with other ministries ... and because it did not have much power or clout at Queen's Park." A Cabinet Office official believed that "the Premier's Council heard from employers that they were not well served by MSD."

## FORMAL DECLINE

Not only did the Premier's Council begin to shift discussions about labour market adjustment policy toward corporatist models in 1989, so did the federal government. Significant changes occurred in federal training policy when the federal government announced the new Labour Force Development Strategy in early 1989. A primary intention of the new policy was "to involve the private sector [business and labour] further in training and employment programming decisions" (Canada. EIC 1990, p. 8). As part of its initiatives, the federal government planned to establish a business-labour national training board to oversee and provide guidance on all national training policies and programs. This board was "expected to mobilize private sector efforts in skills training and encourage the development of a training culture" (Campbell 1992, p. 36). Furthermore, the proposal called for "provincial (regional) and sub-regional boards to be established to guide the operation of training programs at the local and/or sectoral level" (Canada. EIC 1990, p. 9).

MSD was ill-prepared, given its lack of well-structured relations with stakeholders, to respond to the federal government objective of involving business and labour in training policy. The ministry had the expertise to negotiate federal-provincial agreements and purchase training, but did not have the policy capacity to engage business and labour in designing policy. For example, in the fall of 1987 Curling's political staff were dumbfounded when they discovered there were no key client groups for the new minister to meet. MSD had been largely ignored by the business and labour groups that were, in the federal vision, to play central roles in guiding skills training programs. Indeed, one assistant deputy minister of MSD stated that "business did not even know that MSD existed." Thus in early 1989, provincial decisionmakers found themselves — as had been the case in 1985 — in a reactive position vis-à-vis the federal policies position. They realized that MSD was not an appropriate organizational instrument with which to respond to federal initiatives.

It was in this environment that the Premier's Council undertook its study of education, training, and labour adjustment issues. Although its report would not be completed until the summer of 1990, key direction papers from its deliberations were being circulated to senior decisionmakers at Queen's Park in late 1989. Two major themes were beginning to emerge from the Council's work: (i) insufficient coordination among provincial government departments and lack of integration with federal programs for labour market adjustment, and (ii) shortcomings in the educational system, especially the high drop-out rate from secondary schools.

The Council's work criticized MSD's "tendency to focus on youth unemployment ... [which is] out of touch with changing economic and demographic realities" (Premier's Council 1990, p. 116). Furthermore the Council noted that "provincial training programs suffer from a number of other problems" (ibid.). Although the Council was also critical of the two education ministries with somewhat more than half of its 32 recommendations dealing with the educational system and the need for reform, the education ministries were to remain largely unaffected by the call for reform, while MSD was not.

This was principally because at the same time that the skills training ministry reached its lowest levels of power, legitimacy, and prestige in 1989, MoEd attained a high level of these resources. In the words of one central agency official, "the [education] ministry was seen as knowing what it was doing and where it was going." Another person observed that "Shapiro had an excellent relationship with the premier and had expressed strong views on education and training issues." In fact, Shapiro was one of the most powerful civil servants in the government.

As acting deputy minister of MSD, Shapiro's specific task was to "recommend to the Secretary of Cabinet by November 1989 the organizational option(s) that might lead to a better coordination of Ontario's education, training and labour adjustment programs" (confidential report). Shapiro stated that he was under clear instructions that the skills development ministry needed to be eliminated or decreased in size. Shapiro's own background is not unimportant in understanding his response to the request, or indeed why he would be selected in the first place. His position as deputy minister of MoEd meant that he was firmly rooted in the institutional, rather than industrial, training tradition. Prior to becoming deputy minister of MoEd in 1986 he had spent his career as an academic and administrator at several universities.

In tackling the task handed him, Shapiro created an advisory committee, composed of the deputy ministers of MCU, MoL, and the industry ministry to assist him in developing five organizational models for labour market adjustment policy: (i) maintaining the current arrangements; (ii) developing a "super-ministry" by formally merging MSD, MoEd, and MCU; (iii) merging MSD with one other ministry; (iv) divesting MSD programs to a variety of ministries; and (v) creating a new ministry that would combine, among other programs, income maintenance from the social services ministry and training from MSD (Shapiro 1989, p. 6).

With the exception of the status quo option, all the others involved the decline of the skills development ministry. None of the options in the report involved bolstering MSD by transferring programs to it from other ministries. Shapiro discussed the failings of the skills development ministry by saying that "horizontal consensus building within government has not been achieved, the Ministry's delivery system is over-extended ... and insufficient support has been mobilized for the needed improvements in the apprenticeship and training-related income support systems" (ibid.).

In late 1989 Shapiro formally recommended that programs dealing with the training of employed workers be maintained in MSD in preparation for transfer to a proposed Ontario training board, at which time the ministry would cease to exist. Programs dealing primarily with the provision of information and the training of those not employed were to be divested to other ministries, especially MoEd (ibid., pp. 10-12). The recommendation was not among the five options initially developed but it recognized the emerging consensus in the Premier's Council toward establishing a bipartite training board. According to one participant "there was no great enthusiasm for, or opposition to, Shapiro's recommendations when they reached Cabinet; what carried the day was the fact that the senior bureaucrats — Shapiro and the other deputies — were supportive of the report."

In early 1990, 15 of the 29 programs/services of MSD were transferred to other ministries, while the programs remaining at MSD all served employed workers. Of the programs transferred to other ministries: 8 programs and 120 staff went to MoEd; 3 programs/services and 30 staff to the labour ministry; and several smaller programs to four other ministries. The decline of MSD in 1990 caused its annual expenditures to decrease to $243 million from $415 million and its staff to diminish to 454 persons from 609 persons. After the transfer MSD lost one assistant deputy minister position, with the operations and policy division both reporting to one assistant deputy. The consolidation of the divisions assisted in healing some of the schism between the two divisions by reducing the number and influence of policy staff. Remaining with a much smaller MSD were the apprenticeship program and the federal-provincial relations group, the Ontario Training Corporation as well as the other (smaller) industrial training programs. As a result of the recommendations, MSD no longer had programs for youth, literacy, and laid-off workers.

The largest beneficiary of Shapiro's recommendations was the education ministry, of which he was deputy minister at the time the report was written and adopted. He noted "the likelihood that at least in the first instance a new Division will have to be established at Education in order to receive the programs recommended for allocation to that Ministry" (Shapiro 1989, p. 19). The transfer of MSD resources to MoEd increased its staff complement by nearly 10 percent, enabling it to take on an expanded mandate in serving youth and consolidating responsibility for literacy policy. The transfer of programs supported Shapiro's ambition of propelling the education department, as one senior ministry executive noted, "away from a conservative, isolated, protected, school-centred ministry."

In the decline of MSD, the labour ministry regained the labour market research group that was transferred from it (more accurately from the Ontario Manpower Commission) to MSD in 1985, and acquired the Transition and Help Centres programs. The transfer meant that MoL expanded its domain from one primarily of regulation to one involving the provision of some programs to laid-off and unemployed workers. The Youth Start-

Up program went to the industry ministry; the Ontario Summer Experience program to the Ministry of Northern Development and Mines; the Summer Experience program to the Human Resources Secretariat; and the Environmental Youth Corps to the Ministry of the Environment.

MSD's fate had been sealed when Shapiro was appointed acting deputy minister. With both a shared minister and deputy minister, MSD was effectively neutralized, unable to present its own views and proposals. The implementation of Shapiro's recommendations transpired largely within the purview of the same minister and deputy since most of the programs were transferred between two ministries, both headed by Conway and Shapiro. The decline of the skills development ministry in 1990 replicated the situation that existed prior to 1985 when labour market policy was decentralized among a number of ministries. The decentralization of 1990 did not have an appreciable effect on services to clients. The programs that were transferred remained unaltered in their new ministries although the political profile of labour market policy decreased after the diminution of the skills development ministry. In the mid-1990 election little attention was paid to youth and training issues, in part because the province was at the tail end of an economic expansion.

## CONCLUSION

The second half of MSD's life differed from the early years, marking a failure of the organization to address the underlying policy challenge: developing a provincial labour market adjustment strategy. Not only did it fail to develop a grand strategy, it was also unable to rationalize and expand existing programs. The transfer by the premier of community literacy programs to MSD in mid-1987 showed that disjointed incrementalism and lack of agreement about organizational domains continued to be major characteristics of the policy field.

Dissatisfaction within government with respect to training policy by 1989 was not at all dissimilar to that which had induced MSD's genesis in 1985. Ironically, within the space of four years MSD had moved from being hailed as the solution, to being perceived as the problem. There are two striking similarities between the organization's birth and decline. First, and particularly relevant for the next two chapters, is that client groups played no role in either event. Second, although Cabinet was involved in 1989 (unlike 1985), in neither case was there a strategic political vision that accompanied decisions about organizational design.

Two explanations for the decline of MSD fit the observed events: organizational deficiency and competitive pressures. The former postulates that decline came about primarily due to inadequate performance caused by the internal weaknesses in MSD. The later postulates that decline befell the organization chiefly because its performance was hindered by external conditions such as other ministries and central agencies, political shifts, and economic conditions. Organizational size and age, which have also been implicated in decline, can be related to both explanations and are discussed later in this chapter.

The organizational deficiency explanation assumes that conditions and processes internal to MSD were critical in causing its demise. In particular the explanation supposes that the reckless manner of birth, injurious corporate culture, and inappropriate leadership made it impossible for MSD to perform in a satisfactory manner in a difficult policy field. In other words, MSD was designed, structured, and led in such a way that allowed for no outcome other than a defeat in tackling the policy challenges.

The manner of birth of an organization is a legacy that can be expected to influence key aspects of its life (Stinchcombe 1965). For example, legitimacy, prestige, and ultimately performance, are affected by the manner in which an organization is initially created. The stigma associated with being a creature of the previous administration meant that support for the organization waned with political changes. In creating the skills development ministry in 1985, Miller failed to secure sufficient support for the new body from either inside or outside government, resulting in an organization that was very much the whim (or vision) of one individual. The lack of a charter document with a formally entrenched mandate for the ministry contributed to a low level of legitimacy, as well as a general lack of direction.

The rapidity of MSD's birth and insufficient attention by leaders to intraorganizational dynamics resulted in the emergence of two separate subcultures: one for the new policy division and one for the much older operations group. Staff in the operations division resented what was for them a heightened level of control from the policy group. As a result of the schism between the two divisions, the organization as a whole became weak and disconnected.

Leadership is an important factor in influencing organizational performance although it has been difficult to derive direct relationships between leadership and organizational effectiveness. Nonetheless, leaders make strategic decisions on fundamental components of an organization, such as structure, scale of operation, how quickly and aggressively an organization will grow, etc. (Child 1972; Nystrom and Starbuck 1984). Effective leadership results when the skills of leaders are matched with organizational needs and there is little turnover in leadership. In MSD's case, this was not the case: there was a high turnover of ministers, and little match between organizational needs and leadership skills.

The first two deputy ministers were novices and lacked knowledge of labour market adjustment policy, and consequently had scant prestige derived from a successful track record of policy and program expertise. During the early years, senior officials adopted an aggressive and insensitive stance in dealing with other ministries, when logically they should have cultivated relationships with the education and labour ministries even if doing so meant some co-optation of objectives. That this did not occur represents a major miscalculation on the part of MSD's first leaders. As a result, the organization acquired fuzzy boundaries, little credibility, and meager cooperation from others. In turn, MSD officials further avoided cooperative ventures and the ministry hardened its own boundaries.

In Curling, the ministry had a leader with mediation skills who shifted the ministry toward the social policy arena, while what the organization needed at that time was a leader able to procure Cabinet support for the ministry's economic policy mandate. Only in 1988 did MSD's leaders begin to address the internal schism within the agency; however, this was done too slowly and the ministry's strategic plan was not completed until 1989. MSD's strongest leadership, in the sense of commanding Cabinet attention, came during the period of the organization's formal decline when Conway was minister and Shapiro acting deputy minister.

Without a doubt, the leaders of MSD during the five years from 1985 to 1990 made questionable strategic decisions. However, it is unclear whether they made a greater number of strategic errors than the leaders of other ministries during this time. What differentiates MSD from many other ministries is that its interorganizational environment contained other organizations that could undertake some, if not all, of the tasks originally allocated to the ministry. In other words, the margin of error for the skills development ministry was smaller than for other agencies since the fragmented nature of skills training policy meant that it was not a monopolist. The ministry was vulnerable to internal-to-government dynamics and processes because it could not depend, to the same extent as the education ministries, on a well-organized set of stakeholders to express their support.

Tracing the activities of leaders after their tenure at MSD reveals no evidence that those individuals were perceived to have performed poorly. This is *post hoc* reasoning, and it is possible that they learned and improved their leadership qualities based on their experience at the training ministry. Both Tully and Carr, after their tenures as deputy minister at MSD, remained as deputy ministers in other portfolios, while the two assistant deputy ministers remained senior executives with other ministries. Shapiro remained a deputy minister until leaving government in 1993 to become a university president. After his tenure as minister of both MSD and MCU, Sorbara became minister of labour and ultimately a contender to replace Peterson as leader in 1992. All the skills development ministers — Sorbara, Curling, and Conway — were both re-elected in the 1990 election.

The competitive-pressures explanation focuses on external factors in explaining the decline of MSD. Competing organizations are those that compete for jurisdiction and the resources associated with the function (Walmsley and Zald 1973). The "outcome of competition is [the] allocation of functions and resources among bureaus" (Meyer 1979, p. 131). It is rational for organizational leaders to compete if there is a reasonable expectation of altering the existing distribution of domain, function, and resources. In other words, the degree of competition should logically be related to the likelihood that changes can be forced to occur. In view of the history of the labour market adjustment policy field it is reasonable to suppose that the degree of interorganizational competition remained high after MSD's birth.

The study of the contest between organizations has received comparatively little attention for at least two reasons. First, beginning with Max Weber, formal organizations have been viewed largely as rational and efficient structures for organizing activities (Crozier 1964, pp. 175-83). While such a conceptualization does not necessarily imply that organizations do not compete, the "very objectives of public administration — efficiency, economy, and good management — were believed to be incompatible with conflict" (Nachmias 1982, p. 283). Second, when competition has been recognized to be important, especially by critics of the Weberian tradition, it has not been studied as a process. As Selznick first noted, "the dynamics of organizational rivalry — not the mere documentation of its existence" — requires more systematic attention (1957, p.11).

Competition, derived from the existence and evolution of the industrial and institutional training systems and domain overlap, was a long-standing feature of labour market adjustment policy prior to 1985. The Ontario Manpower Commission proposals in 1984 criticizing institutional training and the MCU reorganization (which reduced resources for industrial training) are evidence that competition existed immediately prior to the creation of the skills development ministry. The creation of the skills development ministry channelled competition in a particular direction; namely, between the ministries representing institutional training (MCU and MoEd) and industrial training (MSD).

The skills development ministry faced the highest level of competition from MCU immediately after its establishment in 1985, because both ministries had colleges as delivery agencies. Officials at the colleges and universities ministry feared that MSD might stop using colleges to deliver training programs and fail to protect them in negotiations with the federal government. On the other hand, MSD saw colleges — and by extension, MCU policies — as unresponsive to the training needs of employers. The shared minister placed some limits on the contest and ensured some support by MCU for MSD at the Cabinet table. The ability of Sorbara to resolve several differences between the two ministries from 1985 to 1987 created a false sense of security for the skills development department which was shattered when it received its own minister.

One strategy to increase an organization's life chances is for it to develop linkages to other organizations and institutions that are perceived to have a high degree of legitimacy. Such "external legitimation elevates the organization's status in the community, facilitates resource acquisitions, and deflects questions about an organization's rights and competence to provide specific products and services" (Baum and Oliver 1991, p. 187). During the early years MSD might have paid more attention to cultivating relationships with MCU, which could have become a useful ally, especially since it already had an established relationship with the colleges. Finally, the colleges could have become a grass-roots supporter of MSD since one-quarter of their budgets came from that ministry.

Competition was also fostered by a low degree of regulation and insufficient direction from the centre. The change in government in 1985, the inexperience of the Liberals and the low priority of labour market adjustment policy meant that central agencies were inattentive to training policy prior to 1988. The centre encouraged competition between ministries in order to bring forth the best proposals with Peterson believing that there naturally exists, and indeed should exist, competition between ministries. He stated that "the competition is part of the process [of governing] since each ministry wants to convince you that its approach or proposal is the best."

In reaction to the high level of competition and low degree of coordination, the centre imposed a series of coordinating mechanisms beginning in 1988. These were incremental; that is, one structure was established, its degree of success judged, and then other structures were created. This is consistent with the view that organizations search for solutions to a problem in the neighbourhood of the original or previous solution. This tendency "inhibits the movement of the organization to radically new alternatives (except under circumstances of considerable ... pressure)" (Cyert and March 1963, p. 122). This is also consistent with Lindbloom (1958) who proposed that political action as a whole will be of a gradual or incremental manner. In other words, decisionmakers will "not attempt to consider all alternatives or to ask the grand questions; they take the existing situation as given and seek to make only marginal improvements" (Simeon 1976, p. 577). These structures — interministry committees, joint minister and deputy minister, new Cabinet committee, and the Premier's Council — became increasingly interventionist in the active labour market (MSD's) domain.

The above discussion is not to suggest that overlap and competition between ministries is necessarily dysfunctional. Indeed, duplication and overlap ensure that there are other organizational channels or structures should one fail (Landau 1969; Lerner 1986). Thus, when MSD was unable to deliver, other ministries were available to take over its functions. Although some overlap and duplication between ministries is useful, overlap between 1985 and 1989 in labour market adjustment policy was excessive, leading to ineffective and wasteful policy initiatives and dysfunctional organizations.

Age and size are also factors in organizational performance and decline. With respect to age, the "liability of newness" hypothesis proposes that recently established organizations will face high levels of competition from already established organizations (Freeman *et al.* 1983). A new organization will have difficulty in establishing a domain, and acquiring resources, in an environment in which similar organizations already exist (Wiewel and Hunter 1985) and have become institutionalized (Ritti and Silver 1986). The "liability of adolescence" perspective, proposes that newly established organizations will initially be given the resources and opportunity to prove themselves (Bruderl and Schussler 1990).

Overall, age was a benefit to MSD during its early years, contradicting the liability of newness hypothesis. The newness of the ministry gave it an advantage in that there was no track record against which to judge its performance. MSD's early expansion and success support the liability of adolescence perspective suggesting that organizations do enjoy a period of prosperity immediately after their creation followed by a time of reckoning.

The influence of size on MSD's performance is difficult to judge. Large size may in some conditions confer advantages to organizations such as slack resources or a higher level of power; at the same time, size "should not be equated with success" or performance (Scott 1992, p. 11). Small organizations are often more innovative and successful in adapting to environmental changes than larger ones. According to the liability of the middle, mid-sized organizations are more at risk of decline that either small or large ones (Wholey *et al.* 1992).

MSD was mid-sized both in terms of staff and expenditures — MoEd and MCU had larger budgets, MoL's and MITT's were smaller. In terms of staff, only MCU had a smaller staff than MSD. Clearly a larger size (e.g., funding of more college operations or even its own field delivery offices) would have given the training ministry additional leverage or clout in dealing with the two education ministries and the colleges, but is unlikely to have altered the direction of events. It is likely, however, that MSD was caught to any extent in the liability of the middle: on the one hand it lacked the size (in terms of budget, field offices, staff, etc.) to compete with the larger ministries; but, on the other hand, it was too large to be innovative and adaptable.

The decline of a large and complex organization is not due to a single event or factor. Internal conditions of an organization and the external environment are intrinsically linked. Thus, neither explanation in isolation can explain what transpired. For example, given the early success of MSD, it seems unlikely that faulty implementation, in and of itself, brought about the decline of the ministry. Also, if implementation was faulty to such a degree as to doom the ministry, it would have made sense to abandon the entire enterprise in 1985 shortly after the election. Yet, in 1985, external conditions (political turmoil, lack of a strategic vision, and high rate of youth unemployment) were such that MSD survived.

What can be learned from the life and death of MSD about creating organizations and designing effective coordinating agencies? There are six key lessons that can be extracted from the skills development ministry. The first is the need to do groundwork before introducing a new organization, including a thorough understanding of the policy domain and a clear conception of the organization's function. In other words, politicians need to forge consensus and bring about some alteration in the policy area concomitant with organizational design. A mere shuffle of government organizational boxes is unlikely to bring about improvements in policy or make precarious values more secure. Yet, governments are drawn to new organizations as "a dramatic way to signal a response"; the new organization invariably faces the same problems as the old one (Osbaldeston 1992, p. 67).

A second lesson is that a new organization requires time to coalesce and work effectively. It is more than a chart on the paper; building a corporate culture and consolidating staff takes time. However, governments often do not have the luxury of waiting for results. The importance of the informal organization is central not only to the MSD experiment, but also to the failure of the federal ministries of state in the early 1970s. With respect to those, it was found that "the inevitable challenges of co-ordinating and integrating such activities as policy ... have been compounded by the fact that the Ministry has ... had to house its people in no less than three separate buildings, thus hampering formation of the innumerable informal personal contacts which are necessary to establish a new organization" (Aucoin and French 1974, p. 70). Building stable and non-threatening relationships with other organizations also takes time.

A third lesson is that consideration must be given to how a new organization will be received by existing agencies: in other words, to the "interorganizational politics of accommodation and adjustment" (Brown 1997, p. 71). This implies that there should be a recognition of the "disruption caused by organizational change" (Osbaldeston 1992, p. 50). If there is a history of overlap or lack of coordination in a policy field, explicit steps must be taken to address this in the design of the new organization. For example, the mandate of the new organization must be made clear prior to its appearance, and existing organizations must have some stake in the ultimate success of the new organizational form.

A fourth lesson is that leadership matters, extraordinarily so for a new organization. New structures face a deficit in organizational resources such as power, legitimacy, and prestige by the mere fact that they have no history. Prestigious, appropriate, and proven leadership can reduce the deficit.

A fifth lesson is that support from the centre is important for a new agency. Lack of support from the centre was found to be a critical factor contributing to the failure of the federal ministries of state. Aucoin and French, in reviewing the federal failures, found that "instead of treating the new organization as essentially fully grown once [the] 'birth processes' are over, the central agencies must collectively advise and support the new organization for at least its first two years" (1974, p. 80). The centre along with others also need to have realistic expectations about the performance of a new organization. With respect to MSD, there were unrealistically high expectations that the new agency would solve the fundamental problems of labour market adjustment policy.

The final lesson is that history is important and must be understood by key decisionmakers so that it is not repeated. The change in government in the mid-1980s removed from Queen's Park politicians and their advisors who had the historical knowledge of labour adjustment market policy, organizational design, and the machinery of government. The loss of experienced politicians had a particularly adverse effect on labour market adjustment policy since this field is saturated with precarious values. Consequently, there was insufficient understanding of the dynamics inherent in this particularly turbulent policy area. As a result, the creation of the skills development ministry did little to make the precarious values associated with training more secure.

After reviewing the life and death of MSD's successor in the next two chapters, the final chapter takes up the question of how to design less precarious active labour market policy organizations. The story of the skills development ministry demanded a focus on Queen's Park since the organization's fate was largely sealed by its interactions with other ministries and agencies. The next two chapters take up the role of labour and business which are crucial to understanding the events that followed the demise of the skills development ministry.

# 4

# The Birth of the Ontario Training and Adjustment Board: Forging Consensus

*If the Almighty had consulted me before embarking on the*
*Creation, I would have recommended some simpler.*
Alfonso X of Castile

The election of the first NDP government in Ontario in the summer of 1990 came as an astonishment to nearly everyone, including the newly elected government members of the Legislature. The election result marked a fundamental change in the political environment of the province. The New Democratic ideology and approach to governing was qualitatively different — with its links to labour and social equity groups, emphasis on consultation and mistrust of bureaucrats — from both the Liberals and Conservatives. In appointing his Cabinet, Bob Rae recreated the arrangement of Peterson's early years with a joint minister for the skills development and postsecondary ministries, and a separate one for the education ministry. Each ministry re-gained its own deputy minister.

Although the NDP were initially largely unprepared to govern, it was in labour market adjustment policy that the party was primed to assume the reigns of power. In 1989 and 1990, as the Premier's Council was developing proposals for a training board, the NDP used the Council's work as a springboard in preparing its own election platform. This work was aided by the fact that key leftist policy analysts had contributed to the work of the Premier's Council (Bradford 1998). The NDP envisioned broad training and labour market adjustment policies that included not only employed workers (and business and labour) but also unemployed workers along with equity groups such as women, visible minorities and people with disabilities.

## ENLARGING THE MANDATE

In late 1990 the new Cabinet committee on economic and labour policy established an interministry working group on training and labour force adjustment policy. The ministries of labour (MoL) and skills development (MSD) were given joint responsibility to develop proposals for the new government, and quickly focused on the recently completed work of the Premier's Council. The business-labour consensus inherent in the Council's urging for a provincial training board was attractive for a government that was perceived as being anti-business and for being unduly influenced by organized labour.

The Premier's Council had released its report, *People and Skills in the New Economy*, in July 1990, with the recommendation that "Ontario should establish an Ontario Training and Adjustment Board [OTAB]. This board would be a bipartite management and labour authority to provide strategic direction for the funding and delivery of workplace training and adjustment activities in the province" (Premier's Council 1990, p. 140). The new structure would allow the responsibility for workplace training strategy to be transferred "out of government ministries to the labour market parties where the demand originates, the decisions are needed, and the solutions are delivered" (ibid.).

As envisioned by the Premier's Council, OTAB would be steered by a bipartite board of directors with five business and five labour members with co-chairs from the two groups. Four additional directors would be selected by business and labour to represent other interests along with senior federal and provincial deputy ministers as *ex officio* members. The agency would control all programs remaining with the skills development ministry: apprenticeship and other workplace-oriented training programs. The report also noted that "it is imperative that genuine authority for program and funding decisions be vested in the OTAB" (ibid., p. 142).

By April 1991 two very different visions or models of OTAB had been prepared for consideration by the Cabinet committee: one designed by MSD, the other by the labour ministry. The skills development ministry pushed hard for a small agency focused on providing advice on workplace training with limited responsibility for program administration. Only $25 million of MSD's programs — those already having a strong bipartite co-operative training component, but not apprenticeship — would be transferred to the new organization. A key component of the skills development ministry's proposal was having at least one Cabinet minister on the governing body of OTAB. The ministry argued that ministers would help develop consensus, make certain that government's priorities were represented, "prevent OTAB from becoming another powerful, open-ended demander of public resources," and ensure "high-calibre private sector participation on OTAB by demonstrating a strong political commitment to reform" (MSD proposal, 12 April 1991).

The other model for the training agency — prepared by the labour ministry — was more ambitious, involving the creation of a participatory structure of broad scope and significant devolution of authority from government. A devolution of ownership to major stakeholders was seen as vital to "restore confidence in public training and create an environment conducive to a substantial increase in private sector investment in training" (MoL proposal, 12 April 1991). Unlike the model from the skills development ministry, this one called for the governing board of OTAB to include representatives from social action groups, excluded ministerial participation, and implied the transfer of not only all of MSD's programs but also some from other ministries. Neither proposal was exactly what the Premier's Council had envisioned in 1990. The MSD model contravened the concept that business and labour should play major roles with control of program funding, while the labour ministry's model augmented OTAB's role from one focused solely on workplace training.

The second model was eventually selected by Cabinet for three reasons. First, the more ambitious model had innate appeal to a government committed, as one Cabinet member stated, "to bringing into being cooperative decision-making institutions." The opportunity to emulate the successful European industrial cooperation model proved too appealing compared to the limited and (apparently) unimaginative MSD model. Second, equity issues and a commitment to marginalized groups were central to Cabinet (45 percent of whose members are women), particularly the powerful female ministers at Education, Health, Community and Social Services, and Management Board. This group of influential women was of the view that equity considerations should be inherent in all government decisions, and that a bipartite board would ignore the needs of women, the disabled, and other minorities.

Finally, MSD's model was tarred by the fact that, as one central agency official explained, "the Liberal government had already decided that the ministry would disappear and the New Democrats were not prepared to review this." That under MSD's model for OTAB the ministry would remain largely intact suggested to decisionmakers that its proposal was self-serving. To an extent, the skills development ministry also continued to suffer from its "obstructionist" reputation within central agencies, causing its proposals to be regarded with some scepticism.

An unresolved question about the agreed-upon model was the composition of the training board's governing body. The original bipartite governing model proposed by the Premier's Council was ill-suited for an agency with an expanded mandate. An initial suggestion was for a governing body of equal representation from business, labour, and education/social action groups. However, in May 1991, the composition forwarded to Cabinet was identical to that of the federal Canadian Labour Force Development Board (CLFDB): eight business, eight labour, two education, and four from social action groups. At the Cabinet table some ministers expressed concern that the perspective of those who are not employed (or have not been recently employed), such as social assistance recipients or women who have stayed out of the paid workforce for a number of years to attend to family responsibilities, and the perspective of target-group members, would not carry enough weight on a board dominated by business and labour. These ministers feared that marginalized groups would not have equal access to quality training, and/or that the type of training offered would not meet their needs. Furthermore, both business and labour preferred a bipartite model as proposed by the Premier's Council. Notwithstanding these concerns, the CLFDB model — rather than a completely bipartite or tripartite one — was ultimately endorsed for the provincial agency.

The CLFDB model represented an existing consensus, and according to one Cabinet Office official:

> We made a strategic decision and in retrospect I am not sure it was the best decision ... to just adopt the CLFDB model of representation and hope that by doing so you would speed the consultation process around OTAB along by precluding a huge debate on representation. The fear was that if we did not go with the CLFDB model, some people would sort of point to the CLFDB model and say why are we not doing that, or other people would just open up the whole issue of representation from scratch and you would have to start with all the options on the table (David Wolfe interview, by C. Pervin, 12 July 1995).

The dilemma of how to hold accountable an agency that would spend hundreds of millions of dollars of public monies was a concern shared by politicians and civil servants. At the Cabinet table, ministers expressed concern that the province would be unable to pursue its own strategic policy objectives in the areas of training and labour adjustment, or other objectives (such as employment equity or support for the college infrastructure), which depend on specific training and adjustment decisions, if it no longer had responsibility for training and adjustment policy and programs. Notwithstanding the apprehension around representation and accountability, the proposal to create OTAB was finally approved by Cabinet in May 1991.

At the same time, Cabinet also approved the formation of several dozen joint federal-provincial local training boards across the province. These boards were an attempt to involve stakeholders at the local level and were to be sponsored by the CLFDB, OTAB, and the two levels of government. Local training boards would replace the community industrial training committees that operated in an ad hoc manner in some regions of the province. The development and history of these boards would intersect that of OTAB; however, for the most part their genesis was tangential to that of the provincial agency.

The further development of the OTAB model was to involve significant consultation with stakeholders. In reacting to government proposals both business and labour faced two tasks: adjusting to the changed political landscape after the 1990 election, and finding consensus in their ranks about OTAB. For their part, government officials sought to facilitate consensus and dampen suspicion within, and between, each of the groups, while remaining attuned to the larger political environment.

The Ontario Federation of Labour (OFL) was the most organized of the stakeholders and provided its input concerning the structure of the agency even before Cabinet made its initial decision. The labour federation's objectives were five-fold. First, that ministries continue to have responsibility to deliver programs with the training board's role restricted to designing and evaluating programs. Second, that the government introduce an employer training levy as a payroll tax to fund training programs. Third, that funding to OTAB be allocated in four envelopes: workplace and sectoral training, apprenticeship, labour adjustment, and entry/re-entry. Fourth, that advisory councils be enacted, corresponding to the funding envelopes, to support the new agency. Fifth, that OTAB not be an arm's-length organization so that government employees who transfer to the agency remain full members of the public service and continue to be represented by the Ontario Public Service Employees Union (OPSEU). As discussed below, and in the next chapter, the first two proposals were rejected by government, the third never fully resolved, and the last two accepted.

From the commencement of consultations, frustration began to prevail between government (including both ministers and bureaucrats) and the OFL. In writing to the labour and skills development ministers one OFL official concluded that "We have reversed field ... several times as we wrestled with how" to respond to the proposal to create a training board (Turk letter, 8 May 1991, p. 2). Within the OFL, composed of four dozen unions with half a million members, there was no agreement on training matters: some unions favoured dealing with training as solely a contract issue, others supported sectoral agreements, while others supported institutional responses like OTAB. The decentralized and fragmented nature of the union structure, along with the varying strength of unions and the differences in sectors and regional bases of the unions meant there was no single position on training at the OFL. As Martin has noted: "As an internally diverse movement the OFL had great difficulty with the social bargaining inherent in the OTAB model" (1992, p. 72). The shifting positions of the OFL on key aspects of the mandate and structure of OTAB caused bureaucrats and ministers to become irritated and believe that the labour federation was not supportive of the training board initiative. As the process of setting up the agency progressed these feelings would intensify.

Business associations, on the other hand, were alarmed by Cabinet's decision to expand OTAB's mission, believing that doing so would limit the effectiveness of the proposed organization. Furthermore, business groups feared that a more complex agency would take many years to establish (Wolfe 1997). They preferred a structure with only business and labour representatives accountable solely for workplace training. Notwithstanding the concerns of both business and labour about government directions on OTAB, they continued to participate in discussions around the training agency. Both communities postulated that if they did not mobilize in support of OTAB, the government would "cherry pick" key leaders for the new organization, as was done for the Premier's Council membership. In fact, on at least one occasion, serious consideration was given within government for just such a move.

The impetus in 1991 to create the training agency came not from bureaucrats, business or labour, but from key NDP advisors, especially those with labour movement roots (several of whom had joined ministerial and central agency staffs after the election). Small businesses were wary of government initiatives, especially those of the NDP, while large corporations were ambivalent about the OTAB concept. The private-sector unions — the steelworkers, and communication and electrical workers in particular — were generally sympathetic. These unions were contemplating, if not exploring, a new and more cooperative role for labour, and some already had successful sectoral training initiatives. Therefore, they were favourably predisposed to the concept of a provincial training board. A notable exception was the Canadian Auto Workers which was generally opposed to the concept of "collaboration" seeking instead to rely on collective bargaining as the chief means to advance the cause of workers.

The public-sectors unions, especially OPSEU, which represented the 16,000 college instructors and support staff, felt threatened not only by the OTAB model, but more generally by on-the-job training which would eliminate the role of teachers. For OPSEU, the new training agency was just one way in which "the colleges are being told by employers and governments that the private sector can train present and future workers better, quicker and cheaper" (Hout 1989, p. 37). The existing ideological rift in the labour movement was to expand during the tenure of the NDP and ultimately work to the detriment on OTAB. The one appeal of the new agency to all unions was as a means to enact a "provincial payroll training tax" to be administered by the new body (OFL policy statement on education and training, November 1989).

Senior bureaucrats at Queen's Park were on the whole uninterested in OTAB, partly because of the unsatisfactory experience of the skills training ministry in the 1980s, while training program delivery staff were fearful that an arm's-length agency would threaten their job security. The concept of OTAB terrified the colleges already threatened by federal policies favouring industrial training. To them, the proposed agency loomed as a further attempt to privatize some of their activities.

## INTO THE PUBLIC REALM

The acceptance by Cabinet of the broader model of OTAB in mid-1991 combined with the implied demise of MSD, made Richard Allen, the minister of MSD and the Ministry of Colleges and Universities (MCU), the logical choice to take the lead on establishing the new agency. The acrimonious business-government relationship, especially over changes to labour legislation meant that the labour minister — who might have been the other choice to head the project — was perceived as too partisan (if not too busy) for this task.

After Cabinet's approval several organizational structures sprang into existence to aid in the birthing of OTAB. The first and most important was a small secretariat under a deputy minister reporting to Allen (discussed below). Second, Allen established an external advisory committee drawn primarily from the Premier's Council members to provide advice for, and champion, OTAB. The majority of its members were leaders from business and labour sprinkled with a few representatives from social action groups, along with the business and labour co-chairs of the CLFDB.

Third, a deputy minister's committee was created to ensure coordination across government around OTAB. Its work during 1991 centred on designing the consultation process that would precede the establishment of the training agency. The consultation strategy was prefaced by the belief that, "Given the current economic and political 'climate' ... the number of interest groups and potential impact on public servants and program deliverers, the OTAB consultation process itself will be as important as the information being sought" (confidential document on OTAB Consultation Strategy, 29 October 1991). The emphasis on process, governance, and organizational structures, rather than policy development, would prevail throughout the agency's life.

Economic conditions forced the government to act on labour market adjustment policy while continuing to establish the training agency. In late 1990, the provincial economy began to enter a major recession with unemployment rates and social assistance rates increasing dramatically. Figure 2 shows that the number of unemployed more than doubled to over 600,000 between mid-1990 and mid-1992. At the same time there was explosive growth in the number of persons relying on welfare (Klassen and Buchanan 1997). Figure 3 illustrates the unprecedented five-fold increase, to 240,000, of the number of households classified as "employable" receiving short-term welfare benefits.

To combat these increases, and the concomitant growth of expenditures on social assistance, the government developed a large-scale ($1.1 billion over three years) training and wage subsidy program called Jobs Ontario Training. The program, which began in late 1992, provided up to $10,000 to private-sector employers for the training of each new worker hired from either the welfare rolls or whose unemployment insurance benefits had expired. The program stipulated that workers must be on the regular payroll and remain employed for at least one year. Of the $10,000 subsidy, at

**Figure 2: Unemployment Levels in Ontario, 1985 to 1995 Quarterly Average**

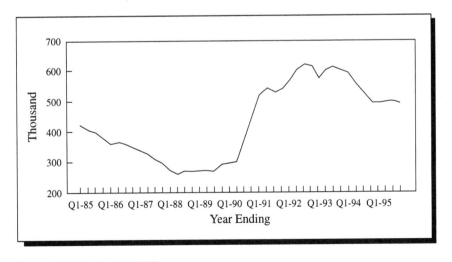

Source: Statistics Canada (1996).

**Figure 3: General Assistance (Employable) Caseloads in Ontario, 1985 to 1995 – Quarterly Average**

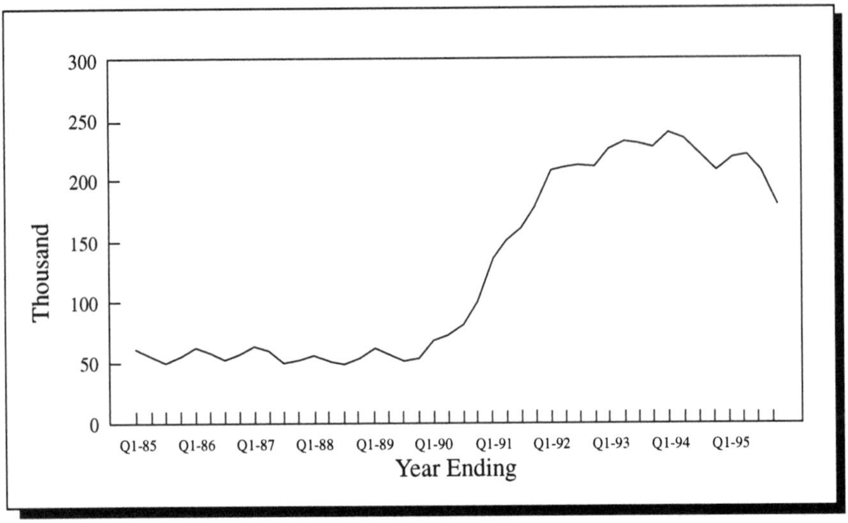

Source: Klassen and Buchanan (1997, p. 334, Figure 1).

least half was required to be spent on training the individual hired, while the other half could be used for firm-wide training. No link was made by politicians between the necessity for a short-term industrial training and wage subsidy program, and the creation of an arm's-length agency. This represented a lost opportunity to craft a more strategic policy vision for labour market adjustment, while at the same time demonstrating the urgency for the establishment of a training agency.

The final organizational structure created to guide the establishment of OTAB as a separate Crown agency was a small secretariat of three dozen seconded staff, primarily from the labour ministry. The prominence accorded to the training agency meant that the secretariat was headed by a deputy minister selected by the premier and reporting to Allen. The deputy came from MoL, and for a while held concurrent positions as an assistant deputy minister at the labour ministry and head of the secretariat.

The influence of the labour ministry in OTAB's birth is a result of the extensive consultation and negotiation mandated by Cabinet with business and labour in building the new agency. The labour ministry, with its mission of mediating between business and labour on employment-related matters, was best equipped for the task. Neither of the education ministries (MoEd and MCU) nor the industry ministry played a significant role vis-à-vis OTAB during 1991-92, with the colleges and universities ministry not even represented on the deputy ministers committee. Educators and trainers were to have minimal roles on the governing body of OTAB and hence largely were frozen out of decision making around its formation. The skills development ministry, meanwhile, operated in a holding pattern, waiting for its demise when its programs would be transferred to OTAB.

The last decision prior to the release of a major consultation document on the training agency was on the status of the staff to be transferred to the new agency. In writing to Allen, the OFL had demanded to know:

> your plans for the Ontario Public Service Employees Union members currently in the provincial civil service and who will be transferred to OTAB. Surely, this government would not want to disadvantage these individuals in any way. This would mean that OTAB must be established as a scheduled agency in which employees remain members of the Ontario Public Service Employees Union, with full rights to pensions, seniority, and bumping privileges within the whole civil service. In other words, a transfer to OTAB would leave the individuals with the same rights and privileges as if they had been transferred to another ministry (letter from Gordon Wilson, 2 October 1991).

Prodded by these concerns and a desire to appease the unions, central agencies created a new type of agency in the fall of 1991 with operational autonomy, but whose staff remained full civil servants. While this "ensured that the government avoided a protracted dispute with one of its key labour market partners, it also continued the shift away from the streamlined type of organizational structure originally recommended in the Premier's Council report" (Wolfe 1997, p. 166). As later events were to prove, by arranging to treat OTAB as a ministry in terms of staffing, rather than an arm's-length entity, the agency's freedom would be curtailed.

The proposal for the training agency finally reached the public domain with the release of the paper, *Skills to Meet the Challenge*, by Allen in November 1991 at a Toronto training centre operated by the United Brotherhood of Carpenters. The choice of locale was inappropriate, despite good intentions, as it seemed to suggest that the very concept of OTAB was unduly influenced by organized labour. Furthermore, the name "brotherhood" seemed at odds with the government's equity agenda.

The paper attempted to splice together: the competitiveness agenda from the Premier's Council and business with labour's view that training is a social right and government's equity plans. It began by noting that "The key to continued prosperity is the development of industries which rely on well-paid, highly educated, highly trained men and women ... At the same time, the achievement of both economic competitiveness and equitable social participation is becoming more and more crucial. The Government of Ontario is convinced that economic competitiveness and a fair, just society for all are linked inextricably" (OTAB 1991, p. i). The paper continued by proposing that only "cooperation by employers, workers, educators, trainers and representatives of community and social action groups" can provide the necessary leadership to cause "dramatic and far-reaching changes to ... labour force development" (ibid., p. 3).

No policy vision was contained in the discussion paper; rather, it argued that: "The government has confidence that when all partners are at the table, OTAB will be able to develop the means to achieve [its] goals" (ibid., p. 21). This, in a sense, reflected the precarious values and associated dearth of agreement within government (and the larger society) about strategic labour market policy. As a result, discussions about the nature of the training agency continued to centre on governance rather than changes to policy or programs.

At times the rationale for creating a training agency was suspiciously similar to that expounded by Miller when the skills development ministry was launched in 1985 (Chapter 2). The training board was justified as not just another layer of bureaucracy, but as a way to simplify and centralize responsibilities that "will actually make Ontario's training and adjustment system more accessible and easier to understand. Right now there are many ministries delivering these services. Business, labour and the employed often find it difficult to determine which ministry should be approached for any given training issue" (OTAB Launch, Question and Answer Sheet, November 1991). Unanswered was the question of whether such a centralization would be any more successful than the one under the skills development ministry. Interestingly, Allen in reflecting on events, recalled being unaware that all the programs to be transferred to OTAB had been located in MSD prior to 1990. This suggests that either bureaucrats failed to inform ministers of past organizational arrangements in this area or that ministers overlooked such information.

While OTAB was to centralize responsibilities, local training boards would decentralize them. During the spring of 1992 a joint federal-provincial consultation panel travelled the province seeking community input for the responsibilities, boundaries, composition, and funding of local boards. The exercise was separate from the OTAB consultations but created confusion in the minds of many about how the proposed local boards differed from the proposed provincial agency.


## SEEKING AGREEMENT


With the release of the public paper, work began on three fronts. First, finalizing the structure of OTAB; second, forging coalitions within, and between, the key stakeholders; and third, mobilizing the bureaucracy to create a new organization.

Discussions on the structure of the OTAB governing body circled around the representation of several groups. Francophones argued that their community had unique training and educational needs and thus required a seat on the governing body of the agency. They were granted one early in the consultations. Municipal governments also lobbied to have a seat on the OTAB governing body utilizing the rationale that municipalities deliver some training programs (for social assistance recipients) and, therefore, were a key stakeholder in training. In late 1992, Cabinet acceded to this request because it seemed consistent with the government's emphasis on partnerships, and avoided alienating municipalities. As a result of the two additional seats, the mandate of OTAB became further diluted. At this time, the education/trainer community began a campaign to increase the number of seats allocated to it on the board.

Still undecided at this time was whether the business and labour co-chairs of OTAB would be full- or part-time. The federal CLFDB full-time co-chairs had quickly become co-opted and lost credibility within their communities because they were perceived as government civil servants by their constituencies. Furthermore, the recently created provincial health and safely agency had revealed that business and labour co-chairs with executive authority were prone to engage in battles. Eventually, the OTAB co-chair positions were made part-time to allow the incumbents to remain credible within their communities and to dilute their power at the agency. Part-time duties were also seen as more attractive in enticing high-profile "blue chip" business and labour leaders to the positions. To compensate for the part-time status of the co-chairs, full-time assistants for the co-chairs were to be selected by the business and labour constituencies. Events still in the future were to reveal the deep flaws of this design.

Forging representative structures within each of the major stakeholder communities proved to be an arduous process for both government and stakeholder participants. Shortly after the release of the discussion paper the major groups — business, labour, education/trainers, women, francophones, visible minorities, and people with disabilities — began establishing steering committees (later called reference groups) which would eventually be responsible for selecting their representatives on the OTAB board of directors.

Some groups, labour and women, already had organizational structures with mandates for labour market policy and training. The OFL had a long-standing education committee, while women's groups had the Ontario Women's Action on Training Coalition. The other groups were less fortunate and had to construct organizational structures that could represent their views on training. The education/trainers group had the most difficulty in organizing, because its members — universities, colleges, school boards, private trainers, and community-based agencies — had no history of working together. Furthermore, these groups expected to be in competition with each other to provide many of the services required by OTAB. Consequently, with only two seats on the governing body, the five disparate groups found it onerous to reach consensus on selecting representatives for the agency's board of directors.

A development that complicated the task of selecting nominees for the board of directors from business and labour was Cabinet's decision in mid-1992 that business and labour's nominees reflect the ethnic diversity of Ontario, and that gender balance of the entire governing body be attained. Business felt that this decree was a nightmare. The OFL, with its male-dominated unions, forwarded only one woman on its initial slate of OTAB nominees, provoking the rejection of the slate by the government.

Not only were the steering committees to select their nominees for the governing body of the new agency, but they were also to help decide its mandate. Drafting the mandate of the training agency, which was to be enshrined in the legislation, proved an early warning of future strains. After months of negotiation, labour, business, and government could not agree on the primary goal of training, whether (i) to increase the competitiveness of employers, (ii) to develop the capacities of workers, or (iii) to achieve labour force equity. This inability to reach agreement caused at least one labour leader to write to Allen that "There is no point being at the table" (Hargrove letter, 20 October 1992). A labour official concluded in an internal memorandum that business had "double-crossed us" in negotiations and that accepting the word "competitiveness" in the legislation "gives us the shaft" (Turk memo, 20 October 1992). For private-sector unions the term "competitiveness" symbolized "cow-towing" to the agenda of business (and of the previous Liberal government).

The issue that took the longest to resolve, and most soured the relationship between government and labour, was the demand by the labour federation that the new agency have responsibility for training in both the private and public sectors. The public-sector unions represented by the OFL insisted that OTAB's programs be available to all workers, including workers in the public sector (OPSEU's response to the proposal to create OTAB, OPSEU, May 1992, p. 3). OPSEU's overriding concern was the protection of its members' jobs, while other unions conceived of training as a social right.

The split in the labour federation between public- and private-sector unions, and the concomitant coalition-building within it, made it difficult for government officials to gain a clear picture of how to resolve this issue. Allen was adamant that public-sector workers were already well served vis-à-vis training by other forums such as sectoral training funds set up by the government in the private and broader public sectors (such as for healthcare workers). Allen was supported by business groups "who did not want money for private sector training diverted to the broader public sector" (Bradford 1998, p. 171). Nevertheless, the OFL continued to argue that "training was training" regardless of the sector in which it took place. The debate lingered until an unsatisfactory and grudging compromise was reached that "a table would be available within OTAB" for public-sector training. The vagueness of the compromise meant that unions continued to press on this matter while government and business kept postponing any action. Reflecting on setting up the agency, Allen has commented that "the one thing I might have done differently is to close off the public sector discussion sooner."

Business groups were no less acquiescent during this time and kept harking back to the exclusion of non-unionized workers from having a voice within the new agency. From the very beginning, the position of the government was that the OFL would represent all workers in Ontario and that it was, in any case, impossible to organize non-unionized workers. Nevertheless, during the final stages of negotiating the training agency's mandate, business wrote to Allen that "it is critical that a mechanism be enshrined to include members of the worker, employer and self-employed constituencies that are not necessarily affiliated with 'identifiable groups' but are a significant part of their communities" (letter by John Howatson, 6 November 1992). In reaction, labour negotiators wrote in internal documents that "business had decided to kill OTAB!" by making a demand that "they know we could never swallow" (Turk memo, 9 November 1992).

Like the OFL, business was having trouble arriving at a consensus, which caused positions taken to the table in talks with government and labour to be later revoked and revised. Notwithstanding these difficulties, only one association, the Federation of Independent Businesses, withdrew from the OTAB process. The withdrawal was less about the training board than about displeasure over changes to Ontario's labour laws which business groups saw as pro-labour (particularly banning the use of strikebreakers) which were passed by the Legislature in early November 1992. In any case, small business had the least to gain from OTAB since its training activities were fragmented and ad hoc.

Although a mandate was eventually agreed upon, the bitterness caused by the battles lingered, especially among the combatants, some of whom would become board members or lead their respective reference groups. Enshrining the mandate, and other key aspects of OTAB, in legislation, had raised the stakes for all participants. The resort to contract negotiation tactics by business and labour was inappropriate and injurious to building trust because with contract negotiations, once agreement is reached, then both sides must, by necessity, resume normal interaction so that the enterprise can function. Given that OTAB did not yet exist, some of the cultural baggage of these negotiations became institutionalized at the board of directors of the new agency.

Government officials underestimated the time required for stakeholder groups to organize themselves and for even basic agreements to be reached among the stakeholders. All the groups felt that government officials failed to understand the difficulties of creating structures that could represent entire constituencies. Groups also came to believe that officials were too involved in "driving the process" often favouring bilateral negotiations, rather than bringing all groups to the table. One labour participant stated that "something we shared with business was the sense that the bureaucrats were running the show." A business official lamented that "our biggest hangup is the forced march we're on" (Scotton 1992, p. 11). Government officials, on the other hand, were frustrated by lack of trust the groups had of government, their constant fear of being disadvantaged vis-à-vis one another, and the infighting within each group.

The third prong of activity during 1992 was internal to government. This work, as with that involving the external groups (outlined above), was coordinated by the OTAB secretariat. The secretariat attempted to engage other ministries in planning for the training agency by constituting several interministry committees. These supported the deputy minister's committee in dealing with human resources and program transfer matters. The secretariat also published an internal-to-government newsletter providing updates to staff throughout the civil service. The claim by the secretariat that "consultation and collaboration with affected ministries have been extensive and have taken place at many levels" was quite accurate (OTAB Cabinet submission, January 1993). This, of course, was in direct opposition to the manner in which the skills development ministry was founded in 1985-86.

The focus of intragovernmental activity was the transfer of programs to the new agency. Although the programs had been identified in *Skills to Meet the Challenge*, some uncertainty remained, especially with respect to labour market entry programs. Furthermore, some ministries doubted that their clients would be well served by the new agency. For example, the community services ministry worried whether its clients (the disabled and social assistance recipients) would be disadvantaged in programs managed by the training board, and that adequate supports — such as income supplements and child care — would be available from OTAB. The concerns of program staff in line ministries, fed by OPSEU, demanded that secretariat officials conduct briefings to explain what OTAB was to be, provide updates, and soothe fears of potential job losses.

## FINAL APPROVAL

One year elapsed between the release of the public paper and the introduction of OTAB legislation in November 1992. This time period was far in excess of the four and six months declared in the paper. The involvement of the stakeholders in drafting the mandate and legislation along with the scale of the undertaking were at the root of the delay.

The speaking notes for Allen's discussion of the legislation with his caucus stated that "All the labour partners have taken part in refining OTAB's mandate and in developing this Bill. This is a unique example of getting those people for whom policies are intended directly involved in policy making." The reality was that no policy making had yet occurred and the only consensus reached by the stakeholders was to sit at the same table. Nonetheless, the premier and Allen continued to believe that strategic and innovative policy would naturally emerge once the corporatist structure was in place.

The legislation went through committee hearings during the first half of 1993. One point of contention was the long-standing demand by education/trainers for three additional seats on the board. The universities in their brief to the committee stated "We appreciate the importance of the major role assigned to labour and business, but ... we find the minor role to which our sector has been relegated to be highly inappropriate ... [I]t raises serious questions about how efficient and effective OTAB can be if those with a demonstrated record of providing training and re-training are not assured of being real partners in this vital process" (Council of Ontario Universities 1993, p. 9). The educational sector, especially the colleges and school boards, continued to harbour fears that the training agency would not be sufficiently protective of the public training and education institutions.

No change was made to the allocation of seats because the government wanted OTAB to be consumer-driven, giving "more representatives to the people who need training and adjustment programs" (*Hansard*, Legislative Assembly of Ontario, House in Committee of the Whole, July 1993, p. 2469). A lesser point of discussion during the hearing was whether organized labour could represent the training needs of unorganized workers, such as those in the agricultural sector. The government argued that there is "a strong record of organized labour representing the interests of all workers" and that in any case "representation among the unorganized...[is] an oxymoron" (ibid., p. 2472). The legislation was finally passed, without major amendments, in July 1993.

The final governing structure was a board of directors with 22 voting members from seven constituencies: eight business, eight labour, two education/trainers, one francophone, one visible minorities, one women, one person with a disability, and three *ex officio* (federal, provincial, and municipal government). The federal and provincial representatives were assistant deputy ministers, and the municipal representative was a social services commissioner from a regional municipality in the greater Toronto region. The voting members were to be selected by seven reference groups and formally appointed by the government. Reporting to the board of directors, but with members selected by the reference groups, were to be four councils: labour force adjustment, apprenticeship, workplace and sectoral training, and entry/re-entry. This structure and the composition of the councils is illustrated in Figure 4. Labour groups believed that a fifth council, on public-sector training, had been agreed upon and continued to press business and government for its formation.

After the introduction of legislation, work continued on establishing the agency and appointing the board of directors. In late 1992 the OTAB secretariat developed plans for an interim governing body to exist prior to the enactment of the legislation. The composition of this body was to be identical to the final board of directors (which could only be legally appointed after the legislation had been passed). The interim body was to develop operational policies and procedures for the board of directors and begin to set priorities for the agency so as to ensure a "running start." The delays in

**Figure 4: Organizational Chart of the Ontario Training and Adjustment Board**

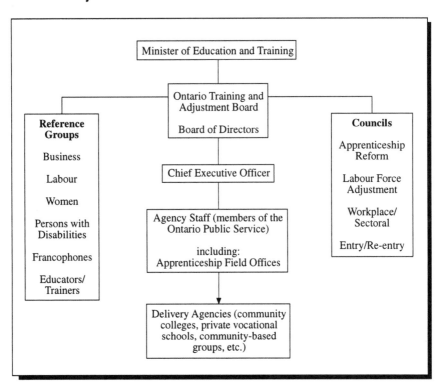

receiving nominations for the board from the various groups, especially labour, and the political pressure to get OTAB operational, meant that an interim body could not be established. This would prove to be a miscalculation.

The programs to be transferred to OTAB were not agreed to by Cabinet until early 1993 when all but one issue had been resolved. The education ministry continued to be adamant that literacy was first and foremost an educational, rather than a labour market adjustment, concern. The ministry vigorously argued that all literacy programs, regardless of whether delivered by school boards or community agencies should remain with the ministry. From the initial discussions about OTAB in 1991, the ministry had expressed concerns about the devolution of programs to an arm's-length agency. In the end Cabinet approved the transfer of the literacy programs, moving them to their fourth home in five years: Ministry of Citizenship, MSD, MoEd, and finally the new training agency.

Of all the programs which had been part of the skills development ministry prior to 1990 only one, the youth entrepreneurship program, was not transferred to OTAB, while the Ontario Training Corporation, which had been created in 1988, was dissolved altogether. The federal-provincial relations function residing within the skills development ministry was not transferred to the training agency but was to remain part of government (located in the ministry to which OTAB would report). Only two OTAB programs, both for social assistance recipients transferred from the social services ministry, were *not* part of MSD in 1989. In terms of policy and program responsibility, budget and staff levels, the new agency was almost an *exact* re-creation of MSD.

A program that was not transferred to the training organization was the short-term Jobs Ontario Training. Early plans called for such a transfer; however, politicians and key bureaucrats eventually concluded that the $200 million a year program was too closely identified with the NDP government and would unduly burden the new agency. Although this was true, without the Jobs Ontario Training program, OTAB was missing a pivotal component of active labour market policy, and especially training, in the province. The decision not to transfer the $150 million (over three years) Sector Partnership Fund to OTAB was far more reasonable than that concerning Jobs Ontario Training, since training was one of several activities supported by the fund. This fund, administered by the industry ministry, provided funding for industrial sectors, such as aerospace, auto parts, plastics, etc., to address research, marketing, training or other requirements (Bradford 1998).

Still undecided in early 1993 was how quickly, and in what sequence, the programs would be transferred to the training agency. Original plans called for the agency to assume program responsibility in a staged manner over a period of two years. Officials at the OTAB secretariat realized that time would be needed for the board of directors to learn to work together as a corporate entity, develop bylaws and acquire a consistent knowledge of the programs, clients, and delivery systems. Nevertheless, the fast-start option was selected by Cabinet to counteract public impatience with the perceived protracted process of establishing the agency. The wholesale transfer of programs would not be to OTAB's advantage.

To assist in the orientation of the members of the OTAB board of directors, an interim group of bureaucrats was created in early 1993 comprising the policy and communication branches of MSD and some staff from the OTAB secretariat. The civil servants approached the task in the same way as briefing a new minister: prepared to pepper the board members with an array of briefings and documents about policies, programs, and government administration. However, there was an inadequate effort to aid board members in working cooperatively in recognition of the disparate backgrounds and skills of these individuals. Furthermore, the civil servants failed to recognize that unlike Cabinet, board members would not be bound by party policy, discipline or solidarity.

The interim chief executive officer of agency, Tim Millard, was also appointed at this time. The term chief executive officer (CEO) was used for the civil servant who headed the agency, albeit chief operating office would have been a more accurate term since the holder of the office did not warrant a vote on the board of directors. Millard was a career civil servant who had been an assistant deputy minister at the labour ministry and most recently headed a bipartite business-labour agency established in the early 1990s to oversee safety standards in the workplace.

In a mid-term reorganization of ministries and a Cabinet shuffle in early 1993, similar to that undertaken by the Peterson government in 1989, a "super-ministry" of education was created. The new Ministry of Education and Training (MET) combined MSD, MCU, MoEd, the OTAB secretariat, and the Jobs Ontario Training program. The new ministry was highly centralized with one deputy minister, rather than the Peterson-era model where separate deputies continued to report to the same minister. It proved ironic that the training agency would now report to the ministry that had been most opposed to its creation, rather than to the labour ministry which would have been far more sensitive to the business-labour dynamics inherent in the new agency. The consolidation of ministries came at a crucial time in OTAB's evolution and would rob the fledgling agency of ministerial attention, while the inclusion of "training" in the name of the ministry was curious given that OTAB, as an arm's-length agency, was to control training policy.

Richard Allen, a university professor before entering politics, had been an unusually committed advocate for, and of, the training agency. As an MPP from the highly industrialized and unionized Hamilton region he had been involved in business-labour issues around worker ownership of enterprises. While minister he was able to devote half his time to OTAB, which would be impossible for the new minister of MET. Allen's demotion to junior minister responsible for international trade eliminated a passionate advocate for OTAB from the Cabinet table. Shortly after his demotion, the agency lost its other key supporter when David Wolfe, executive coordinator of the Cabinet Committee on Economic and Labour Policy, returned to academia in the summer of 1993. Wolfe had published on training policy (see Wolfe and Yalnizyan 1989) and had been involved in writing the training section of the Premier's Council report in 1990.

The mid-term Cabinet shuffle signalled the end of the government's learning curve and the beginning of a greater emphasis on fiscal policy with Rae having "asserted his determination to move close to a balanced budget before the end of his term" (McBride 1996, p. 78). At this time there was, as one minister expressed it, "concern that there was too much going on and a great deal of energy spent on many initiatives." This anxiety also led to the downgrading of the role of the Cabinet committees, which were seen as generators of too many initiatives and pressures for spending, along with the consolidation of ministries. After the shuffle the government's policy agenda became more focused, leaving, as analyzed in the next chapter, the training agency adrift on the sidelines.

During the spring of 1993 there was still some doubt as to whether OTAB would come to exist at all. The new deputy minister of the training and education ministry (who now had responsibility for the training agency) described the emerging agency as "very, very fragile" at a Cabinet Office briefing. The government's "social contract" proposals to contain public-sector costs by setting aside the provisions of collective agreements in the public sector had infuriated the unions, who in turn refused to name representatives to the OTAB board. Finally, with the passage of the OTAB legislation in July 1993 and the naming of the last members of the board of directors, the organization finally moved closer to reality.

The official launch of OTAB, including the public announcement of the board of directors, took place in July 1993 in a nondescript boardroom in a government complex at Queen's Park. That this event did not occur in the Legislature or in the community reflects the low political priority that the agency was now accorded. With the official transfer of programs from the Ministry of Education and Training (including the former MSD programs), the labour ministry and other ministries, and the first board meeting in September 1993, the training agency had at long last come to life.

## CONCLUSION

The establishment of OTAB was an attempt to institutionalize the active involvement of interest groups, primarily business and labour, in training and adjustment. The agency was an ambitious undertaking given the historical lack of interest, and different ideologies, of business and labour in playing active roles in this policy area. The size and governing structure of OTAB was significantly affected by the political power shift that occurred in the 1990 election. The organization attained a much broader social policy mandate, including providing training for marginalized groups such as social assistance recipients, than the skills development ministry had from 1985 to 1990, or than was envisioned by the Premier's Council in 1990.

In some ways the creation of OTAB was the fulfillment of the work begun by the Ontario Manpower Commission in 1984, representing a return to preeminence of the labour ministry and industrial training in the policy field. The limited role for education and postsecondary education ministries in OTAB's birth, and the fact that only two seats on the board of directors of OTAB were allocated to the education community — despite strong lobbying for more seats — denoted a (temporary) loss of power by institutional trainers. Of all the ministries involved in the establishment of OTAB, the education ministry was the most cautious, expressing repeated opposition to the devolution of policy to the agency, and in the end, was granted oversight of the new agency.

The manner of OTAB's birth reflected the political landscape of the early 1990s, especially the new government's emphasis on equity and consensus. The creation of OTAB also shows that government was not the arm of any single interest group. The expansion of the mandate of OTAB to include equity concerns clearly derived from the preferences of ministers, not bureaucrats, business or labour.

Cabinet, perhaps because of inexperience, failed to realize the extent of its ability to act independently while retaining the commitment to OTAB from stakeholders. In setting the mandate and governing structure of the agency, too much emphasis was placed on trying to obtain consensus and gaining cooperation from all groups. Unilateral action by Cabinet on some matters, such as membership on the board of directors and objectives for the agency, would not have caused key groups to withdraw from participating in the creation of the training agency.

The expectations of OTAB, both within government and outside it, were substantial and at odds with the structure of the agency. Politicians believed that the training board was a means to draw new energy into labour market policy, develop creative initiatives and promote a training culture. Some labour groups believed that the agency would ultimately result in the introduction of a training tax or levy with workers having access to more and better training. Business groups conceived of the agency as a means to aid in keeping businesses competitive, especially in light of the recession of the early 1990s and the rise in global competition. However, the organizational structure and programs of the agency — other than the, not insignificant, addition of an outside board of directors — diverged little from that of the failed skills development ministry.

Setting up the training agency differed fundamentally from the fiat used for MSD: OTAB was conceived outside government, decisions about it were made by Cabinet, there was significant consultation inside and outside government, and the agency's mission was enshrined in legislation. The differences in the manner in which the two organizations were established can be explained by the proposition that organizations "learn" from their past (Hedberg 1981; March 1988). Organizations learn by "encoding inferences from history into ... the forms, rules, procedures, conventions, strategies ... around which organizations are constructed and through which they operate" (Levitt and March 1988, p. 320). The changes in processes and strategies "are independent of the individual actors who execute them and are capable of surviving considerable turnover in individual actors" (ibid.)

The fashioning of OTAB was an attempt, notwithstanding that in some cases different actors were involved, to avoid the mistakes of MSD's creation. Organizational learning, however, relates "not to outcomes — for example, improvements in performance — but to processes" (Scott 1992, p. 110). If this is the case, the organizational learning inherent in OTAB need not necessarily result in improved organizational performance, only in new procedures and strategies. The next chapter examines the performance of the new agency and the extent to which its actions strengthened the values surrounding training.

# 5

# The Death of the Ontario Training and Adjustment Board: Incompatible Values

*We tried, we tried to make it work; but it was an impossible task.*
Member of OTAB board of directors (1996)

In September 1993, 22 men and women charged with $450 million in public spending met for the first time in a downtown Toronto boardroom. Who were the 22 individuals? Not one had been a member of the Premier's Council or the minister's advisory committee. Fewer than half of the labour directors were elected union officials, the majority were union staff members or retired from the union movement. The business board members were either small business owners or human resources managers in large corporations, while the equity representatives had long histories of advocacy on behalf of their constituencies. A university professor and a middle manager from the teachers' federation were the education/trainer representatives. Three of the eight board members from both business and labour were women, and one man from each slate was a member of a visible minority. Including the three non-voting *ex-officio* members (federal, provincial, and municipal government), 12 of the 25 directors were women.

## GREAT EXPECTATIONS

The level of experience, prestige, and understanding of public policy and complex organizations of the OTAB board members differed greatly from those on the Premier's Council. The Council's members were overwhelmingly white males comprising the business, economic, and educational elite of the province. Among its members were the presidents of IBM of Canada, GM of Canada, Weston Foods, General Electric of Canada and Dofasco, the president of the OFL and several of the major unions as well as university and college presidents.

The method of selecting the OTAB directors strongly influenced the type of individuals appointed to the agency. Complete authority over selecting board members, other than meeting the government's equity requirements, rested with the steering committees and, not unexpectedly, the selections became highly political. Often the persons ultimately selected were compromise candidates whose major qualification was their acceptability to all factions within their reference group. An example of how these factors played out is the labour slate. In the original OFL slate, Fred Pomeroy, the executive vice-president (later president) of the Communications, Energy and Paperworkers Union of Canada and a member of the Premier's Council, was the nominee for co-chair. The nominee for full-time associate co-chair was D'Arcy Martin, a policy advisor from the same union who was highly respected for his work in dealing with government and business on training issues.[1]

Both individuals were strong and experienced supporters of the social bargaining and the "expansion of the range of co-operative activity" inherent in new bipartite and tripartite training institutions (Martin 1995, p. 102). The other unions in the OFL, however, opposed having the two key labour positions on OTAB being occupied not only with advocates for corporatist institutions but also members of the same union. As a result, Pomeroy and Martin were replaced by safer choices, who would be more accountable

---

[1]Martin describes some of his experiences around OTAB in *Thinking Union: Activism and Education in Canada's Labour Movement*, pp. 97-108.

to, if not controlled by, the OFL and the other unions. Glenn Pattinson, a vice-president in Pomeroy's union and chair of the labour federation's education committee, became the compromise nominee for the labour co-chair of the training agency. Pattinson, having less power and prestige, would have less independence to act than Pomeroy. To placate public-sector unions and increase the number of women in the labour slate, Erna Post from the Public Service Alliance of Canada replaced Martin. These choices, according to several Cabinet members, caused dismay in the NDP caucus where many had sought to recruit Pomeroy and Martin for the new agency. Donald Green, the business co-chair, was the semi-retired head of a mid-sized multinational auto parts company with prior experience on a number of public-sector and charitable boards.

The two co-chairs had only moderate prestige and influence within their fractious communities, making it tough for them to provide effective leadership for OTAB. Neither had sufficient prestige and power to have qualified for membership on the Premier's Council. At a personal level, they had little in common on which to build a relationship since they came from distinct social classes and moved in separate realms. When in the same room, the immaculately groomed upper-class Green and the rumpled working-class Pattinson made an odd couple.

In addition to selecting the members of the board, the business and labour reference groups had also selected the assistants for the co-chairs. The status of these positions in the organizational structure was never clarified and would lead to acrimonious conflict. Because all staff positions at OTAB were part of the civil service, the two jobs were made equal in classification and salary to middle management. The title of associate co-chairs was chosen by business and labour in an attempt to confer more power on the positions than originally intended by government officials. The ill-defined function of the two positions combined with the discrepancy between the formal status and power (low) and salary (relatively high) of the positions would create disputes and misunderstandings. Furthermore, those who were to become the administrative leaders at the agency would come to see the positions as interfering with their role in running the agency on a day-to-day basis.

From the agency's inception, the nature of the associate co-chair positions had been subject to divergent assessments. The business co-chair was of the view that the position should be equivalent to that of vice-chair "with responsibility for running the agency while the co-chairs ran the board meetings." Both co-chairs assumed that the assistants had full authority to act in their absence. However, for education ministry officials, the positions were no more than executive assistants to the co-chairs and, in fact, ministry officials refused to meet the associate co-chairs on substantive matters unless the co-chairs were also present.

Like the now defunct skills development ministry (MSD), OTAB was comprised of approximately 560 staff and had an annual budget of $450 million (which remained virtually unchanged during its life). Table 5 shows the spending of MSD, OTAB, and the Jobs Ontario Training program from 1992 to 1996. Of OTAB's total budget, just over $400 million was transferred to delivery agents, primarily the colleges which received 65 to 70 percent of all transfer payments, with the majority of the remainder going to community agencies. The apprenticeship and FUTURES programs accounted for half the funds transferred to the colleges. Table 6 shows a breakdown of the agency's spending, which was similar to that of the skills development ministry.

The lack of a corporate culture, or even trust, among directors became apparent from the minutes of the first board meeting in September 1993. The suggestion by the two co-chairs that Millard, with whom they had been working since July, be appointed CEO on a permanent basis was not well received by the equity groups. The equity directors were, in the words of one, "totally outraged" at the lack of process inherent in the suggestion and ascribed it to an example of "the old boys network." For the equity directors, obtaining the best CEO meant following a formal recruitment process.

Also, at the first meeting, in the words of one co-chair, "directors were in an uproar about having been assigned by the co-chairs to board subcommittees" because they felt that they should be free to choose which subcommittees to join. Eventually the carefully balanced membership (equal number of business and labour directors and two equity directors) for six subcommittees was assented to, even though the goal of equal representation from groups on each committee resulted in a misalignment of directors' expertise and duties. A director recruited to fill the quota on the finance committee recalled that "I didn't understand all the numbers and anyway I wasn't interested in them."

**Table 5: Expenditures for Selected Ministries, Agencies and Programs, 1992 to 1996 (millions of dollars)**

| Year | MCU | MCSS | Ministry MoEd/MET | MITT | MoL | MSD |
|------|------|-------|----------|------|-----|-----|
| 1992 | 3,296 | 8,314 | 6,414 | 281 | 236 | 252 |
| 1993 | 3,396 | 9,413 | 6,197 | 362 | 262 | 252 |
| 1994[1] | – | 9,242 | 9,340 | 385 | 180 | – |
| 1995 | – | 9,338 | 8,741 | 480 | 144 | – |
| 1996 | – | 8,920 | 8,974 | 360 | 133 | – |

| Year | OTAB | Jobs Ontario Training |
|------|------|-----------------------|
| 1993 | – | 98 |
| 1994 | 455 | 237 |
| 1995 | 442 | 197 |
| 1996 | – | 250 |

Key: MCU = Ministry of Colleges and Universities
MCSS = Ministry of Community and Social Services
MET = Ministry of Education and Training
MoEd = Ministry of Education
MITT = Ministry of Industry, Trade and Technology
MoL = Ministry of Labour
MSD = Ministry of Skills Development
OTAB = Ontario Training and Adjustment Board

Notes: The data in the tables is presented by fiscal year. Therefore, the data for 1992 is from 1 April 1992 to 31 March 1993 and so forth for all other years.
[1]In 1994, MCU and MoEd were consolidated into the Ministry of Education and Training. Significant changes were made to government accounting procedures in 1994, meaning that 1993 figures cannot reliably be compared to those of past years.

Source: Ontario. *Public Accounts*. Various years.

Without shared values or even trust, board meetings became lengthy affairs fixated on minutia. The November 1993 meeting began with a lengthy discussion, as noted in the minutes, of: "how detailed the [board] minutes should be and whether directors should be named in the minutes when they raised matters for consideration. It was suggested that the degree of detail in the minutes [be] related to the use being made of them ...

**Table 6: Ontario Training and Adjustment Board Program Expenditures, 1994**

| *Annual Expenditures by Function (in millions of dollars)* | |
| --- | ---: |
| Employment preparation (FUTURES, etc.) | 167 |
| Apprenticeship | 79 |
| Foundation skills training (literacy, etc.) | 69 |
| Programs for employed workers | 61 |
| Adult training | 32 |
| Adjustment programs (Transitions, etc.) | 29 |
| Corporate functions | 12 |
| Local boards development | 6 |
| **Total** | **455** |

Source: OTAB Financial Statements for the fiscal year ended 31 March 1995, Office of the Provincial Auditor of Ontario; and OTAB/COFAM (1995*a*).

If they were for the purpose of the reference groups more detail was required. Reference groups expect reports from the board meetings" (Draft Minutes, 16-17 November 1993, p. 3-A-3).

Although attempts were made by Millard to institute "off-line" approaches, such as subcommittees, to deal with some items, these did not work because many directors did not feel at ease unless involved in all steps of decision making, no matter how minor an issue might be. When disagreements arose, the recourse was to focus on process. One director explained that "many meetings dissolved in a prolonged discussion of whether the process had been right either at the board or at a committee level. Going back to first principles or driving the board back to first principles was a standard method on the part of some board members." The size of the board and the desire for nearly all members to speak on most issues meant that much time was spent in "going around the table." Most frustrated with the emphasis on process were the business directors, many of whom ran small businesses. One stated that in his company he was used "to making decisions quickly and not worrying about process."

Also apparent at the first meeting was the propensity of labour directors to "caucus" before, during, and after meetings. Caucuses are a fundamental feature of union culture in which the concept of unity is crucial, since a "union is a group of people who have joined together to protect each other and to work together for the benefit of everyone in the group" (Newman 1993, p. 17). This strategy was soon adopted by the equity representatives who realized that to be effective they needed to operate as a group and eventually business also emulated the practice, notwithstanding that it was initially foreign to the business directors. During meetings, groups would increasingly find it necessary to caucus, such that rooms had to be made especially available for this purpose. Instead of coalescing as a whole, the directors began to form ideological camps.

Only one attempt was made to assist the heterogeneous board to build trust and a common vision of its task. In October 1993 the board held a two-day retreat outside Toronto which resulted in some team-building. However, the benefits of the retreat withered away because no further forums were planned; an error attributable to the co-chairs and the CEO. As matters remained, board members had no informal opportunities to share information and learn about each other's values and beliefs. Although more attempts to forge informal bonds among board members would likely not have altered the eventual outcome, they might well have contributed to the emergence of less bitter camps within the board.

There emerged three distinct cultures within the board of directors: one held by labour and equity members, one by business, and the last by the civil servants. The culture of the labour and equity groups emphasized unity and faithful allegiance to a cause, or at least to the reference groups. In contradiction, the culture of the business members accentuated rapid decision making, entrepreneurship, and a focus on efficiency. Finally, the culture of the civil service (discussed in depth later in this chapter) stressed loyalty to the political masters and hierarchical decision making.

In November 1993 an unprecedented policy shift shook the labour movement of the province when the Ontario Federation of Labour (OFL) convention voted to work to defeat the NDP government. This action was taken in response to the government's "social contract," which infringed on existing collective agreements, to freeze wages and force workers to take unpaid "Rae days." This was unacceptable to many public-sector (and some private-sector) unions, especially when decreed by a social democratic government. To protest the attack on labour's traditional ally, some unions walked out of the annual OFL convention, fracturing the labour federation and consequently intensifying the difficulties the labour members of OTAB had in working together and acting autonomously, if not boldly.

Selecting a permanent CEO became a major priority for the board of directors in late 1993 and early 1994. Doing so exposed one of the flaws of government's acquiescence to the OFL's demand that the training agency's employees remain civil servants. The CEO position was classified at the assistant deputy minister level which limited the compensation that could be offered to around $100,000. Millard had been willing to remain and indeed had formally applied for the job, but asked for deputy minister status which would augment his prestige and somewhat increase his compensation and benefits.

The request to alter the classification of the position to deputy minister status was not supported by the education and training ministry and ultimately rejected by central agencies. Ministry officials were concerned that elevating the CEO position to deputy minister status might result in corresponding demands by the co-chairs for privileges similar to those of a minister, since deputies report to ministers. Furthermore, having the agency's CEO at the deputy minister level meant parity with the deputy at the education and training ministry (MET) which was problematic to ministry officials who saw OTAB's administrative leader as reporting to their deputy minister. Central agencies were trying to restrict the number of deputies and did not weigh the management challenges of the agency as equal to those of a ministry. Furthermore, the secretary of Cabinet, who made the final decision, was inexperienced and uninformed in managing the civil service, and the loss of Wolfe and Allen deprived the training agency of strong advocates at the centre.

Not raising the compensation level of the CEO position had four results. First, it deprived the agency of a talented and charismatic leader. Second, Millard's departure in early 1994 created a leadership hiatus, delaying the agency's progress in developing policy and reforming programs. Third, it limited the number of persons who would be interested in replacing Millard, especially from the ranks of senior civil servants and executives accustomed to private-sector salaries. Fourth, it suggested that the training agency was no longer a priority for the premier (and Cabinet) since the OTAB secretariat which had had only a handful of staff, had warranted a deputy minister.

The reference groups, which had grown out of the steering committees, proved to be another troubling aspect of the agency's structure. In addition to selecting directors, reference groups were to act as a link between the training agency and the seven constituencies. By 1993, each reference group developed its own unique structure and culture; for example, the women's reference group had seven subcommittees, the persons with disabilities group six, while the business group had one. Each group developed its own mission statement and communication strategies, hired staff for specific functions, and reimbursed members for expenses. Debating the level of funding for reference groups was an ongoing OTAB board item, especially because equity groups clamoured for additional money. The seven reference groups received in excess of half a million dollars annually for their activities, with equity reference groups receiving a greater share than the other groups (whose members had more resources). Although this was not a great deal of money, critics began to point to this expenditure as an example of unnecessary bureaucracy and wasteful spending associated with the new agency.

The powerful influence of the reference groups on directors was a major reason for the board's inadequate performance. As one director observed, "as long as the people sitting on the board were simply advocates for their own reference groups the board could not work as a board, but when members stepped out of the role and began working as effective board members they risked losing the support of their group." Consequently, some directors did not aspire to be anything other than mouthpieces for their constituencies.

Directors who sought to act with some degree of independence found, in the words of one, "that I could never negotiate on any major points because of my reference group." One of the agency's CEOs expressed his frustration at the "unalterable mandates" that board members brought with them. All directors suffered from this problem, and the education/trainers group was neutralized by the powerful institutions they represented. The chair of the education/trainers reference group noted that: "Our committee is very concerned with the concept that the decisions made at the board

level are made in a fashion that each of our reference groups has the opportunity to have good input into the decisions ... and that those are not being
brought back to us after they have been made. We don't necessarily want
to be a rubber stamp reference group" (OTAB public meeting, video, 14-
15 June 1994).

A senior OTAB official recalled a director calling him at home pleading
to "come explain matters to my reference group before they kill me!" To
gain a sufficient degree of autonomy from reference groups directors needed
either to have sufficient power or prestige within their community (which
most did not) or to spend considerable time educating their community
(which was impossible given their full-time jobs). A further difficulty for
the equity directors was to overcome their sense of marginalization which
arose from the historical exclusion of equity concerns in labour market
policy. For the most part they were unable to do so, continuing to act as
advocates rather than realizing they were now decisionmakers "at the table."

Dave Cooke, the education and training "super-minister" with responsibility for OTAB, regarded the agency differently from Allen, his predecessor. Like Conway in 1989-90, he found that training and labour market
adjustment policy were always last on the list of ministerial priorities,
meaning that OTAB received considerably less support than it had under
Allen. Shortly after assuming his portfolio, he reached the conclusion that
"OTAB did not have a prayer of working" because too much attention had
been paid to special interest groups in the governance structure and that
"trying to create a United Nations was a mistake." The new deputy had
only a fraction of time for the agency compared to that devoted by the
OTAB secretariat deputy. Finally, government priorities changed from
institution-building and expansion in 1990-92 to fiscal constraint and program reductions thereafter (McBride 1996).

Negotiating the memorandum of understanding between OTAB and MET
exemplified the uncertain relationship between the agency and the ministry. The memorandum took nearly a year to negotiate and showed that
keeping the training agency accountable remained in the forefront of government priorities. The initial document drafted by ministry officials sought
to micro manage OTAB's affairs, for example, requiring it to submit to the
ministry all correspondence received or sent to the Ombudsman, Ontario
Human Rights Commission, and other bodies. Not surprisingly the co-

chairs, in writing back to the minister, argued that the proposed memorandum "put the agency under direct government control to a greater degree than expected given previous descriptions of the agency as 'autonomous', 'independent' and 'arm's-length'. It is understood that the agency must remain accountable to you as the responsible minister, and that some limitations on our activities are necessary. In our view, the controls described in the government proposals go well beyond what is necessary in this regard" (letter to Cooke from Green and Pattinson, 27 January 1994). Thereafter a flurry of paper exchanges on the memorandum consumed unnecessary effort from both parties which culminated by mid-1994 in a compromise that pleased neither party. Consequently, there was, as one assistant deputy minister concluded, "no loyalty and buy-in to the final document."

The major disagreement between the two organizations was the degree of autonomy of the training agency. Ministry bureaucrats wanted OTAB to be responsive to, and supportive of, government policy initiatives, fearing that directors would be more accountable to their constituents rather than government priorities. Their view was that coordination of government policy initiatives was difficult, or impossible, if the agency was not directly involved in government decision making. Reflecting on OTAB, one senior ministry official observed that "there was never a good understanding at OTAB about what arm's-length meant." This comment applies, conversely, equally to MET!

Many OTAB directors and officials regarded the agency as sufficiently arm's-length to preclude becoming marred in specific government initiatives, believing that the very rationale for the organization was that "it was not government." Their view was that a great deal of effort had been expended on governance mechanisms to ensure that OTAB would operate effectively as an autonomous institution. Their position, as summarized by one director, was that "you can't have it both ways."

Ministry officials, used to dealing with institutionalized organizations such as universities, colleges, and school boards, could not understand the protracted discussions and decision making associated with the agency's board of directors. Indeed, MET officials had no prior history or experience in dealing with corporatist structures and thus the new agency remained an anomaly in the ministry's universe of advisory bodies such as the Education Relations Commission, Ontario Council on University Affairs, Advisory Council on Special Education, College Standards and Accreditation Council, and others.

The allocation of funding for OTAB programs was just one area in which there came to exist differing views on the agency's autonomy. Neither the legislation nor the memorandum of understanding referred to spending envelopes corresponding to the major program areas (such envelopes had been suggested by labour groups during the discussion leading to the formalization of the training agency). Nonetheless, senior ministry officials operated under the premise that OTAB was unable, without approval from MET, to reallocate funds between the four program areas. As a result, the agency was uncertain to what extent it could reallocate program budgets without seeking government approval.

The training agency's most notable contribution during the first phase of existence was in the creation of the local training boards. The establishment of the 25 boards had been placed on hold until OTAB was functioning as the agency was to become the fourth partner in their establishment. In discussions with the education and training ministry, the Canadian Labour Force Development Board (CLFDB) and the federal government, OTAB argued for larger, rather than smaller boards, and became fixated with equity issues. The business directors wanted the local boards to have executive powers (to fund programs) while the labour and equity directors believed their local constituencies were not sufficiently sophisticated to operate autonomously. OTAB played a role in the creation of local boards because its directors were not public servants and thus were perceived to be effective in representing the concerns of business, labour, and equity groups in negotiations with the governments about the structure of the local boards. However, as noted by a senior official involved with local boards, the boards "could have been brought into being without OTAB" because the key players in establishing the boards were the federal and provincial governments.

The first phase of OTAB's life culminated with what was, for optimistic observers, a triumphant public meeting in a downtown Toronto hotel in June 1994. In attendance were the members from all the reference groups, nearly 200 members of the public, the education minister, and the premier. The standing-room only turnout suggested to some that a critical phase in reducing the precarious values surrounding training and labour market adjustment had at long last been reached in the province.

By this date the agency had been in place for nine months and counted its major achievements: making a presentation to a royal commission, aiding in establishing local training boards, "planning a new approach to literacy training," and formulating a French-language service strategic plan (remarks by Pattinson, 14-15 June 1994). At the public meeting there were no proposals from the agency to its constituencies, merely a forum for various groups and individuals to bombard the board members with their concerns and requests for services. Directors responded to questions by suggesting that OTAB is, or would be, responsive to all issues and groups. However, missing was a visionary program of how the agency would effect change and build on the process that emerged.

From the public meeting, the board received two conflicting messages from politicians: to produce visible results quickly and to get the process correct. Cooke, after completing his prepared remarks, said: "I want ... to reiterate the importance that I think we all have to place on communication with the people in the province. OTAB is a real risk for the government. I think a risk with incredible payoffs for the economy and for jobs ... However, people in the province ... are waiting to see some of the visible signs that OTAB is up and running" (OTAB Speeches, 14-15 June 1994).

The premier, speaking after Cooke, talked of the precarious status of the agency, but focused on the importance of process: "I'll be very candid with you ... there are a lot of people in government who are very sceptical about [OTAB] ... Their view was ... it's probably better for us, in terms of managing this thing politically and overall, if we just take hold of it ... I've certainly expressed concern at a number of meetings that this is all taking quite a lot of time. But, I think it's important that we get the process right" (ibid.).

Released shortly after the public meeting, the agency's annual report was a glossy six-part document, including messages from the CEO, questions and answers by the co-chairs, an OTAB map, etc. To meet the demands of the equity directors the report was made available in braille, audio, and large print. The splendid presentation, like that of the public meeting, only seemed to confirm to many that OTAB had nothing to report other than its existence. To others, OTAB seemed poised to finally take flight: its new permanent CEO was about to take the reins, the memorandum with ministry had been signed, many internal operational issues had been resolved, and the public meeting had attracted hundreds of participants.

## MUDDLING ALONG

The new CEO, Garth Jackson, who took office in the summer of 1994, was a compromise choice designed to appease all parties, including the deputy of the education and training ministry who had sat on the hiring committee along with the co-chairs and one equity director. Jackson had a lifetime of experience at the community colleges, most recently as president of a small northern Ontario college. His management style was very different from the personal charisma, long experience in government, and knowledge of business-labour relations that Millard had relied on. Jackson was a consensus-builder; low key, soft spoken, and accustomed to the collegial culture of academia. In part, he was recruited to appease the colleges who continued to be, in the words of one observer, "paranoid about what OTAB would or would not do." From the beginning he was hindered by not having served in the civil service; and thus was foreign to a culture that valued interpreting the political winds correctly, adhering to hierarchies and processes, and preventing, at all costs, embarrassments to one's minister.

The interregnum of several months between CEOs, combined with the increasing withdrawal of the co-chairs from providing leadership, created a vacuum into which stepped the associate co-chairs. This was the case especially for the business associate co-chair, who was thrust into a larger role by Green's disengagement from the OTAB board. Green had become consumed with his business affairs and was, in any case, most effective in the initial phases of ventures. His deputy, the associate co-chair, sought to acquire formal authority to direct agency staff, once claiming the title of executive vice-president, although such a position did not exist in the organizational chart. Such behaviour provoked quarrels between Jackson and Green, souring the relationship between the CEO and the business caucus.

The councils or permanent subcommittees reporting to the board of directors originally suggested by the OFL had became enshrined in the OTAB legislation. From the beginning, the agency's staff were wary of these bodies, fearing that their establishment "could be a complex, time-consuming and contentious issue for the Board to take on" (OTAB briefing note on councils, 12 September 1993, p. 2). Although the legislation did not require councils — only providing the option of creating them — the OFL, whose idea the councils were, and groups not represented on the board of directors felt that the councils were necessary to allow their concerns to be fully addressed.

The increasing antagonisms among the board of directors and the board's inability to reach consensus on policy matters meant that referring the contentious issue of how to reform OTAB programs to the councils was appealing. Consequently, four councils (apprenticeship, workplace and sectoral training, entry/re-entry, and labour adjustment) were established to review programs and recommend changes. The composition of the apprenticeship and workplace and sectoral training councils was identical to the OTAB board, while the other two were fully tri-partite (equity groups, labour, and business). Not surprisingly, hatching the councils raised some of the same dilemmas as setting up OTAB. For example, the first slate of nominations from reference groups (other than labour) for the councils was rejected by the OTAB board because, as noted in an internal staff memo, "the equity groups had concerns about the representativeness of each others' slates and about the representativeness of the business slate."

Labour and equity directors, along with their reference groups, wanted council members to receive income replacement for time served on the councils. This required Cabinet approval and created angst about why members of advisory bodies were being compensated, and why the compensation was income replacement rather than the more typical per diem stipend. Cabinet was uneasy about setting a precedent for the multitude of other provincial agencies, boards, and commissions. OTAB argued that "councils will be playing more than a purely advisory role. They will be assuming a key role in the program reform process by performing comprehensive program reviews. Councils are being established as a means of analyzing the strengths and weaknesses of OTAB's programs and services ... with the validity that can only come from the users" (OTAB briefing note, 24 August 1994). The remuneration package was eventually grudgingly approved by Cabinet, but raised questions within and outside government about why the agency was intent on creating four new mini boards.

The councils were given 18 months to forward recommendations to the program review subcommittee of the board of directors. The first meetings of the councils held in early 1995 encountered the same birthing contractions as those of the OTAB board in 1993. The budget for the councils was one million dollars a year in addition to support provided by OTAB policy staff, further fuelling criticism that spending on consultation and administration was increasing without concomitant results.

With the councils responsible for program reform, and those reports not being expected until the second half of 1996, the funding of reference groups continued to be a major point of debate at meetings of the board of directors. In late 1994, the discussion continued as:

> Some board members expressed concern that under the [finance] committee's proposal their reference groups would get less funding than they received in the previous year. For the women's reference group, the funding for operational costs under the "equalization" component was considered inadequate; the budget underestimates the size of the mailing list, costs, and the salary of support staff. Overall, the amount was not commensurate with the reference group's mandate to reach the whole province and to address systemic barriers faced by women who have historically been marginalized. The women's representative indicated she could not support the Finance and Audit Committee's proposal without discussing it further with her reference group (Draft Minutes, 18-19 October 1994, p. 2-5).

Rather than taking flight, OTAB seemed to be perpetually grounded.

Dissatisfaction with OTAB's performance began to be expressed by several groups: MET, the business caucus, individual members of the board of directors, and the Opposition parties. At the end of 1994, the ministry sought to provide greater direction for the agency by developing a policy framework that would "provide OTAB with an overview of the government's broad priorities and fiscal environment to be taken into account as OTAB undertakes its mandate. In some cases, the Policy Framework may provide specific directions to OTAB" (*A Plan for a Policy Framework* for OTAB, MET, 6 December 1994, p. 1). The project was not instituted but is an illustration of the discontent felt by ministry bureaucrats about the agency's inaction and their attempts to influence, if not control, the agenda.

The business caucus, in reviewing the first year of OTAB's existence, noted an overall frustration for a variety of reasons, primarily the lack of speed in decision making and excess discussion at the board. In order to overcome these and other shortcomings, the business directors suggested that the co-chairs begin to represent the entire board, not just their constituencies, that the role of the associate co-chairs be expanded; and that modifications to programs be undertaken immediately.

In 1993 the Conservative Party in its position paper on education proposed a re-assessment of OTAB to increase efficiency and reduce expenses (Ainslie 1993). Furthermore, the party noted an imbalance of power on OTAB due to the overrepresentation of organized labour and special interests. Notwithstanding these criticisms, the party did not yet question the overall existence of the new training agency.

By late 1994, the directors of OTAB pondered improving their decision-making structure: namely, creating an executive committee. Because the board met only once every two months, and often deferred matters, decision making was sluggish. Fearing that an executive committee would become the real board within the board and undermine the role of the full board, the concept failed to obtain the consensus required for approval. Instead, ad hoc working groups of board members began to be utilized, but without formal powers these failed to expedite decisions.

Although there was a voting procedure available to the board, it was never resorted to because doing so was perceived as signifying a failure of the bargaining and compromise inherent in corporatism. If a vote had been called on a motion it would have required the support of at least five labour directors, five business, and two others in order to pass. The board of directors was successful in steering clear of a formal vote, but at the cost of avoiding many decisions altogether.

Some of the dissatisfaction of the business caucus (and other directors) about OTAB's performance became directed at Jackson. Millard's leadership style had been much better suited to the culture of the business directors than Jackson's aversion to conflict, and his consensus-seeking, soft-spoken approach. As the business co-chair noted: "Tim [Millard] was very good at stepping in to help the board come to a decision while Garth [Jackson] just wanted to slide under the table. He was the wrong person at the wrong time." Another business director was of the view that "we would have accomplished more without him ... he never produced anything ... he should have been fired."

The harsh judgements of Jackson's performance fail to consider that during his tenure OTAB faced significantly greater challenges than during Millard's. The initial excitement of constructing a new agency had waned, the demands from government for a reform of programs were increasing along with a higher degree of scrutiny than during the start-up phase, while the directors had failed to coalesce into a corporate entity. The escalating claims by the business associate co-chair for a hand in running OTAB presented a further irritation and, along with Green's withdrawal, caused relations with the business caucus to degenerate. At the same time, Jackson was the wrong person because his expertise and skills did not match those required for the position. His leadership style was better suited to that demanded by a highly institutionalized organization than a young agency. Ironically, Jackson would have been a better administrative leader for a skills development ministry in the 1980s: expert on training, well connected with the colleges, and a team player. His major accomplishment at OTAB was keeping the relationship with the education and training ministry from deteriorating, a not insignificant triumph given the antagonisms and misunderstandings that had developed.

As 1994 proceeded, central agencies became more and more concerned about controlling government expenditures, including asking ministries to reduce their expenditures. Like all ministries and agencies funded from general revenues, OTAB had to face some budget cuts; however, because its employees were civil servants, the agency faced a second round of cuts directed solely at staffing expenditures. In-year budget cuts are not uncommon to ministries which, with their highly centralized decision-making structure, are able to find budget savings within the four to six weeks imposed by central agencies. OTAB, however, with its time-consuming decision-making process had difficulty meeting the deadlines; thus causing fresh frustration at the education ministry, which represented the agency in Cabinet along with other central agencies.

Many OTAB program staff found that operating as an agency, rather than a ministry, allowed them a greater flexibility in operational policies, such as reducing the time to flow funds and process invoices. The transfer of programs to the agency had been done smoothly and all the Toronto staff were located in the same building from the start. An OTAB staff culture developed quickly, in part due to Millard's efforts, which incorporated a sense of "not being part of a ministry" and also because senior officials had learned from the dysfunctional intra-organizational warfare at MSD. During the early months there was a strong *esprit de corps* and sense of excitement among staff. Unlike MSD, there were no disruptive conflicts between staff and policy disputes, and those that did arise —

such as the degree of autonomy that OTAB should adopt — did not become personalized. A senior OTAB official, in analyzing the role of his bureaucratic colleagues, concluded that "at MSD we were the authors of our misfortune because some of us acted like school children; at OTAB it was the board of directors."

As 1994 progressed, OTAB staff increasingly lost faith in the board of directors, which bred distrust between staff and the board. Staff felt that the board demanded inordinate energy, in comparison to a minister, for minimal return. Some members of the board were attracted to operational aspects (such as the lease payments for OTAB buildings) which staff deemed distracted the board from strategic issues and caused unnecessary work. More serious for the staff was their belief that board members violated a cherished value of the civil service by sharing confidential documents with their reference groups. In retaliation, OTAB staff began to stamp all documents submitted to the board as "draft." The interregnum between Millard and Jackson meant that power had flowed to the board (and to the associate co-chairs), escalating the intrigue and ideological battles at the board. This further complicated the work of staff.

The staff-board relationship remained difficult because neither party had a history of working with the other, or an understanding of the tensions that always exist in such a relationship. Some, if not many, board members had distrusted government for many years and relished the opportunity to finally order bureaucrats about. In some cases, board members of quite disparate ideologies and backgrounds had this as one of their few shared frames of reference. Other board members had wildly unrealistic initial expectations about how to guide a public agency of OTAB's size, imagining staff to be secretive, unresponsive to board directions, and, as one stated, "almost seeming to want to derail OTAB." In return, staff came to believe that the board was unpredictable in its decision making and suspicious of staff. As a result of the mutual mistrust, staff became uncertain of the extent they could or should exercise leadership on policy issues. Jackson explicitly addressed the gap between staff and board when he joined the agency: "It is also clear that staff are very committed. While they are creative and innovative, however, they are holding back because they are anxious to be sensitive to the board's right to establish policy. Measures or changes important to our clients may not be taking place" (Draft Minutes, 9 August 1994, pp. 2-10).

The organizational structure of OTAB remained largely unchanged throughout its life although there was a minor restructuring in early 1995 when Jackson created four vice-president positions: board support and policy, internal services, workplace preparation programs, and workplace support programs. These positions were essentially a renaming of existing portfolios, but they did provide the agency with a private-sector guise and held the promise of further organizational innovation. The training agency might have benefited from arrangements to have advisors and researchers from the OFL and unions, along with individuals of business and equity associations working side by side with OTAB staff (as proposed by the Premier's Council in 1990). However, the restrictive civil service human resources regulations, along with the OPSEU contract, under which OTAB operated, prevented such secondments or other related innovations.

In the spring of 1995, the NDP began to prepare for the election that had to be called later that year. For its platform, the party hastily assembled "a new strategy creating and expanding training, education, and work experience opportunities for young people" (Minister of Finance 1995). For the most part, this initiative involved small increases to funding levels for OTAB youth programs and minor program modifications, which were developed by central agencies without input from the training agency. OTAB made a strategic error in not being proactive and having a series of policy initiatives ready for the NDP government to consider in early 1995, while at the same time preparing for a possible new government.

The agency's future began to hinge on the outcome of the election. The Liberal Party was explicit in its criticism of the agency, stating that:

> OTAB puts training decisions in the hands of a centralized structure far removed from the needs of local workers, employers and communities. It diverts $14 million a year from training towards its own bureaucracy. It is far behind schedule, creating confusion as to how companies will get training programs for their workers. Most important, it has become so bogged down in discussions over process that it has failed to come up with any new or creative programs for the unemployed ... Our first step will be to: scrap the highly centralized OTAB and replace it with a strengthened system of the existing local training networks that deliver the training local communities want and need (Ontario Liberal Party 1995, pp. 15-16).

The Conservative Party's *Common Sense Revolution* platform did not mention the agency, but OTAB policy staff concluded that under a

Conservative government "it can be assumed that the agency will feel the impact of general reductions in government size and spending" (OTAB briefing note, Policy Staff 1995).

To the optimists, the second year of the agency's life showed that it had surmounted the perils of becoming institutionalized and was beginning to achieve its objectives. To others, this phase demonstrated that the agency was mired in process and unable to fashion policy or alter the status quo.


## DESTRUCTIVE WARFARE


After the election of a Conservative government in June 1995, the agency entered a period of immobility as it tried to decipher the new government's position vis-à-vis it and the active labour market policy in general. In mid-August, OTAB was notified that a review of the province's training system, including OTAB's role, was underway and it was directed to immediately terminate the four councils and within three months provide its recommendations on labour market adjustment policy.

During this time, ministry of education and training bureaucrats worked hard to save the local training boards, because they represented a federal-provincial initiative and furnished provincial decisionmakers with a channel to business and labour. Not coincidentally, retaining the local boards made OTAB less necessary. John Snobelen, the new minister, quickly agreed to retain the local boards. The brisk decision, and the fact that OTAB weathered the initial rounds of budget cutting in 1995, left some believing that the new government would continue the agency as well, although in an altered, and improved, form.

During September the board of directors struggled to decide what policy proposals it could submit to the government. Labour and equity directors argued for a visionary document stressing the utility of active labour market policy, while business directors wanted a document with concrete designs for restructuring the agency and rationalizing programs. Frustrated by the inconclusive nature of the board discussions, the business caucus tabled its paper containing a series of proposals: reducing the size of the board to ten members, operating with one chair, using a simple majority to make decisions, augmented preparation of board members and greater autonomy for OTAB. The paper also called for a $57 million spending reduction (13 percent of OTAB's budget) by eliminating the Ontario Skills Development Offices and the Transitions program. Furthermore, literacy programming was to be returned to government since "using OTAB as a 'repair depot' for dropouts from the regular [school] system is inefficient and costly" (Creating an Effective and Focused OTAB, OTAB business caucus, 13 September 1995, p.8). Finally, the paper advocated for the agency to be eliminated altogether once a training culture had been sufficiently entrenched in the province and the private sector accepted responsibility for training.

The reaction by the other board members to the proposal was explosive with business directors branded as traitors bent on sabotaging the agency. The use of the term "employees" rather than "labour" in the business document infuriated the labour caucus, and the accent on competitiveness also angered the equity groups. The insinuation that eventually OTAB might no longer be required outraged the groups as well. Several days after the meeting, the labour and equity directors wrote to the business caucus and to OTAB staff that "we are extremely disappointed at the way in which this paper was distributed. It demonstrates a lack of respect for the trust and the goodwill we thought was present ... While each individual caucus has the right to make others aware of their proposals, the short-sighted way in which this was done serves to undermine the Agency. Consequently, we are not prepared to discuss this paper at any future board or committee meeting" (Memorandum to business caucus from labour/equity directors, 25 September 1995).

While the board of directors was imploding, the new minister was receiving advice from his own officials, including his deputy who recommended that "OTAB be repatriated" to the ministry because of the agency's lacklustre performance. At the same time, as part of a review of all government agencies, boards and commissions, the Premier's Council was eliminated. Although in the 1990s it had turned its attention to other policy fields, the recommendation to establish OTAB represented the Council's most notable achievement and by 1995 the Council remained the only group that might have championed the training agency with the new Cabinet.

The OFL was also beginning to review its commitment to OTAB. After the election, at least one public-sector union petitioned the labour federation to reassess its participation in OTAB in light of the new government's elimi-nation of the councils and income replacement for local board members. In fact, it appeared that labour might withdraw from the agency to protest the new government's policies. At the same time, notwithstanding the ac-tions of the business caucus, business groups in the larger society contin-ued to be largely uninterested in OTAB. In 1995, the business associate co-chair observed that "members of the [business] reference group still need to be persuaded of the importance of being involved in OTAB, local boards and councils" (OTAB briefing note, March 1995).

The open rift in the board made reaching consensus hopeless and conse-quently staff began to take a progressively larger role in policy develop-ment. The report finally agreed upon by the board and forwarded to the education ministry in November 1995 was largely crafted by staff based on some of the work of the councils. Unlike the business caucus paper it did not deal with the structure of the agency nor did it include financial information; it merely described how programs might be rationalized and realigned with greater emphasis on sectoral training initiatives.

Unable to get the board to heed its warnings for change, the business caucus began to contact Cabinet members directly to solicit their support for modifications to OTAB. By doing so, caucus members assumed that they were salvaging the agency by bypassing the ministry and central agency bureaucrats who were bent on destroying it. However, the attempt at an "end run" caused a colossal row with ministry bureaucrats which only fur-ther impaired OTAB's case for continued existence. The MET deputy min-ister angrily told the business co-chair: "You don't do end runs in government."

The board meeting of January 1996 failed to get a quorum because the business members boycotted it. By this time the agency was listing dangerously with inadequate leadership from the board or Jackson; even so, the business caucus escalated its efforts to convince Cabinet of the value of a restructured training agency. In February 1996 a paper was pre-pared by the business caucus for Snobelen. The proposals in the document were more ideological and less balanced than the earlier paper, calling for five of the ten board members of a reformed OTAB to be from business with only two from labour, and the chair selected by business and govern-ment. The paper also proposed significant cuts in staffing and programs.

Ironically, the paper contained innovative policy proposals — such as for an Ontario registered training savings plan, and the establishment of an integrated labour market information system — which OTAB had been unable to generate.

The training agency's fate was decided by Cabinet early in 1996, but kept confidential until April 1996 when, buried in an announcement of program reductions across government, was the decision about OTAB. The agency was to be dissolved to attain "a more focused, simplified and cost-efficient training system" (Statement in the Legislature, summary of MET business plan, p. 2). All programs were to be transferred to the education and training ministry and the training budget decreased by $77 million (17 percent) in 1996-97.

As part of the funding reduction, several programs — Transitions (for older workers), Social Service Employment Program (for social assistance recipients), Ontario Skills (subsidies for business) — were eliminated, as was the Jobs Ontario Training program. These terminations were the first substantive changes to training policy since 1987 when MSD had introduced the Transitions program and Help Centres, other than the short-term Jobs Ontario Training program. As a result of disposing of the programs, labour market adjustment policy became focused on supporting economic competitiveness, re-creating the emphasis of MSD's early years.

Looking back to the dissolution of OTAB in late 1995 and early 1996, all members of the board of directors expressed outrage about how they were treated. One noted that "what lives on is the frustration and anger about the final few months." The labour and equity directors felt betrayed by the business caucus, while business directors declared that their attempt to rescue the agency was misunderstood by the other directors and ignored by politicians and bureaucrats. All directors considered themselves shabbily treated by the Liberals who initially sought the advice of stakeholders, the New Democrats who had asked them to join the training board in 1993, and the Conservatives who summarily dismissed them in 1996. The disinterest in the training agency by the new government in 1995 came as a shock to directors unaccustomed to changes in political power. The lack of a debriefing or final board meeting left unresolved feelings, created ill-will toward government, and failed to consolidate the gains, even if small, from the OTAB experiment.

## CONCLUSION

OTAB was a more innovative organizational structure than the skills development ministry incorporating the devolution of significant executive authority to groups outside government. The model of a private-sector agency was developed during the tenure of a centrist party in booming economic conditions and political concern about economic competitiveness. The board came into being during the tenure of a social democratic party emphasizing process and equity, whereas the end of the experiment came from a Conservative Party bent on reducing the size and complexity of government.

What did OTAB accomplish? The agency did bring together two groups — business and labour — who historically have engaged in conflict. However, the fact that government, social equity groups, labour, and business agreed to participate did "not mean that there [was] unanimity within or among" them (Dehli 1993, p. 99). OTAB was a devolution of decision making and administration from the hegemony of the state; albeit, in many ways the state remained firmly in charge, because the agency had little latitude in making strategic decisions.

Wolfe (1997) argues that OTAB was crucial in establishing local boards, and although the agency did play a role in this undertaking, it was far from a crucial one. The local boards could have been created without OTAB and indeed continued to exist without it. OTAB was successful in managing existing programs: administrative improvements were made to youth and literacy programs, while equity groups and social assistance recipients were well served by existing programs.

Like the skills development ministry, OTAB failed to design a provincial labour market adjustment strategy; furthermore, it showed little promise in even rationalizing existing programs. It was ineffective in increasing the amount of training undertaken in the workplace, or even fostering debate on this matter. As with its predecessor, two major explanations for these failures are most likely: the agency's design was flawed, and the external conditions made success impossible.

The flaws of the OTAB model were the large size of the board, the lack of orientation and education for board members (and staff), the cumbersome decision-making structure, and the tenuous role of the associate co-chairs.

With 22 voting members the board of directors was sluggish in decision making, especially given the reliance on consensus. Most directors had no previous experience in leading a mid-sized corporation, were unfamiliar with the role of director, and inexperienced in working in bipartite or tripartite forums. Because insufficient effort was devoted to the orientation of directors and staff, neither group functioned as well as it could have with directors failing to build trust and staff treating the board as they would a minister (which is not surprising since staff continued to be government civil servants).

The structure of the board gave the co-chairs insufficient authority to make decisions and facilitate consensus because they had no recourse to additional power — such as an executive committee or the ability to remove disruptive board members — to ensure the effective functioning of the board. The positions of associate co-chairs were ill-conceived, combining aspects of line and staff responsibility. Yet, by virtue of the fact that the positions were full-time, and the incumbents were appointed by the reference groups, significant informal power flowed to the positions. However, without formal power and with undefined reporting responsibilities, the positions became disruptive to the operation of the board and agency.

With respect to leadership (as was the case for the skills development training ministry) the question is: Could the outcome have been different had leadership been different? The answer is definitive: No! No matter how skilled the individuals it seems impossible that OTAB in its existing configuration could have succeeded, yet in spite of this, the termination of the agency might have been modified (leaving a more positive residue) had there been different leadership at OTAB and in government. The example of the Canadian Labour Force Development Board which met a fate similar to that of OTAB in 1999 is illustrative. Its board's demise was more orderly and planned while OTAB's was haphazard and left a bitter taste for many of those who had invested time and energy during its life.

The co-chairs were not strategic thinkers, had insufficient prestige among their constituencies, lacked knowledge in leading an agency of this size and type, and were further handicapped by their part-time status. Many board members were unaccustomed to working with a CEO and failed to understand the impact on organizational performance of the board-CEO relationship. Furthermore, the co-chairs saw their role as guiding the board of directors while the CEOs saw theirs as managing the internal operation of the agency, leaving no one to communicate with OTAB's broader constituency and the public at large.

The failure of OTAB did not taint the leaders associated with it, suggesting (at least in the view of others) that no strategic errors were committed. Although Allen's status in Cabinet was reduced in 1993 he did become minister of housing later in the NDP mandate, while Cooke was re-elected in the 1995 election. The deputy of the OTAB secretariat continued as a deputy in the line ministries, while Millard was promoted to deputy minister of the labour ministry. Jackson became an assistant deputy minister at the education and training ministry after OTAB's dissolution. The board members remained in their various private-sector capacities with the exception of the associate co-chairs who were dismissed from the civil service and faced periods of unemployment.

The key stakeholders for the skills development ministry had been other ministries and the colleges; for OTAB its stakeholder groups were MET and the reference groups. As with MSD, OTAB's relationship with the education ministry proved to be a difficult one, highlighting the long-standing competition between industrial and institutional training. The education ministry officials were not supportive of the agency, failing to understand its unique needs and although the NDP Cabinet championed the creation of OTAB, it failed to nourish the agency after 1993.

The power of reference groups to select and recall board members created a dissonance between board members' responsibility (to labour market policy) and accountability (to reference groups) leaving directors with little leeway to exercise the discretion that is fundamental to providing effective leadership (Guest 1962). In any case, the internal dynamics of stakeholders caused ill-suited members to serve on the board and stymied decision making at the agency. Lastly, the reference groups operated in isolation from each other, so that in the selection of the co-chairs no consideration was given to the compatibility of the two leaders.

Unlike MSD, there is no sense that OTAB operated more effectively early in its life, since it was apparent from the beginning that the board of directors would not be able to develop and agree on strategic policy. Could OTAB have worked given more time? Some participants argued that the extraordinary nature of the agency, along with the historical hostility between business and labour, required that more time elapse before judgements could be made about performance. Yet, there is no evidence that strategic decisions on labour market policy — and the necessary trade-offs between business, labour, and equity groups — could ever have been reached by the board.

What lessons can be learned from OTAB about designing organizations to make these less precarious? The nine lessons presented below flow directly from the OTAB experiment. Chapter six takes up the theme of how to improve organizations and policy by examining the lessons — for theory, policy and practice — from both the skills development ministry and the corporatist training agency.

An obvious lesson from the attempt to establish OTAB is that it takes time to bring into existence a new organizational form, especially one based on a corporatist model. Time pressures on the part of politicians who required that the agency be operational sooner rather than later resulted in sub-optimal decisions such as not staging the transfer of programs or having an interim board of directors.

The second lesson is that OTAB's mission was too broad. The agency should have been focused solely on workplace training as originally proposed by the Premier's Council. By adding equity groups, the OTAB model "took a 'giant leap' forward relative to other international counterparts" (Bhyat 1995, p. 100). A leap for which all parties were unprepared. Responsibility for achieving greater equity should have remained in government rather than being devolved to an arm's-length agency whose major stakeholders had little experience or interest in equity issues.

Related to the previous lesson was the fact that the agency was too large. Smaller organizations are easier and faster to establish than larger ones while carrying less risk for all participants. The large size of the training agency increased the expectations surrounding it within the NDP government (Miller 1993, pp. 350-54). For business, labour, and equity groups, OTAB's size caused them to be more vociferous in defending their interests than might have been the case in a leaner agency. The size and complexity of the agency meant that it was nearly impossible for board members to understand the many programs for which they had responsibility, much less to make strategic decisions (Young and Briers 1996, pp. 4-6).

The fourth lesson is that in a corporatist entity all partners must sense there is equality among them in terms of influence. The lengthy haggling between the OFL and government on public-sector unions gave the (perhaps erroneous) impression to other groups that labour was unduly influencing the design of the agency. When the OFL executive committee became the *de facto* reference group for labour, it further seemed that labour had a privileged role in OTAB, causing the agency to become synonymous with the NDP government and therefore subject to shifts in political power.

The fifth lesson is that forcing business and labour to have an ethnic diversity and gender balance in their representatives for OTAB, which did not exist in their leadership, was inappropriate and meant the best people were not nominated to the board of directors of OTAB. To function most effectively, OTAB should have been composed, as was the Premier's Council, of individuals with high levels of prestige and credibility within business and labour. This would have meant that the OTAB board might have been composed largely of white males, which was unacceptable to the NDP Cabinet.

The sixth lesson is that considerable efforts are required to assist board members, reference groups, and government officials to build trust and to work in a cooperative manner. The emergence of a division of labour is a key feature of cooperation; however, the board members never trusted one another enough to allow for an appreciable division of labour in their duties. Furthermore, ritual and ceremonies are "important in maintaining social cohesion and cooperation" (Argyle 1991, p. 125). Again, there was no blueprint for this to occur, either formally or informally and the board members remained strangers whom fate had brought together. Joint trips to workplaces, training centres, and other jurisdictions would have allowed a greater understanding and *esprit de corps* to function among the heterogeneous directors.

The seventh lesson is that governments are not adept at allowing active labour market policy to be made by private parties, or even providing adequate forums for this to occur (Haddow and Sharpe 1997). As a result of the concerns by ministers and bureaucrats, the final model of the agency saw it firmly tethered to government, and to the ministry most concerned with the devolution of responsibility to an arm's-length agency. That OTAB employees continued to be full members of the civil service meant that the agency did not have the autonomy required to fulfil its mandate. By not sufficiently emancipating OTAB from government directives, the agency's mission became unclear. If OTAB were truly the progeny of business and labour, these groups would have had a greater stake in the agency's performance.

The eighth lesson is that government, not stakeholders, should have selected at least some of the business and labour leaders to sit on the board of directors. By doing so, politicians could have bypassed some groups, such as small business and public-sector unions, working only with those unions and business associations that were interested in corporatist training policy. This would have avoided fruitless debates, such as the one on public-sector training, while forging OTAB as a smaller organization with a narrower, but clearer, mission. Explicitly focusing the organization on private-sector training would have ensured its insulation from some of the fallout over the social contract. Over time government might have given constituencies more power to suggest members for the board of directors and considered expanding its mandate into the broader public sector. This matter is taken up further in the next chapter.

The final lesson is that organizational death, like birth, requires attention and planning. The complete dissipation of trust, among board members and between the board and government, in late 1995 might have been avoided if politicians and government bureaucrats had been more attuned to the nature of the commitment to the agency that had evolved among board members. Given the preeminence of process in OTAB's birth, the eradication of OTAB was accomplished with a lack of even rudimentary civility, including ignoring the importance of the ceremonies and rituals that should accompany organizational death (Hall 1991, p. 193).

# 6

# Conclusions: Precarious Values and the Future

*We should all be concerned about the future because*
*we will have to spend the rest of our lives there.*
Charles F. Kettering (1876-1958)

The preceding chapters traced the struggles of Ontario governments from all political stripes to develop and coordinate active labour market policy between 1985 and 1996. Much of the struggle centred on designing organizational structures and the two agencies created to develop and co-ordinate policy — the Ministry of Skills Development (MSD) in 1985 and the Ontario Training and Adjustment Board in the early 1990s — proved wholly inadequate. The training ministry was a traditional line ministry in structure, while the training board was an ambitious corporatist model involving business, labour, and equity groups in decision making. Although the organizational structures failed to survive, their policies and programs have endured to some extent.

## RECAPITULATION

The MSD's function was to shift policy toward greater reliance on indus-trial, rather than institutional, training and to rationalize the numerous programs that had arisen in the policy field. After an early success in consolidating programs for youth, the ministry floundered, in part due to deficiencies in its design, inattention from central agencies, and misjudgements by its leaders. Over time, a lack of domain consensus decreased the ministry's legitimacy and it was unable to garner sufficient support for its mission from other government departments. By the late 1980s it became apparent to the Liberal government that the ministry could neither adequately develop, nor coordinate, labour market adjustment policy.

In 1989, the ministry began to be dismembered with the objective of replacing it with a bipartite (business and labour) agency charged with coordinating training for employed workers. The agency's ambitious design was partly in reaction to the failure of MSD, and incorporated a significant devolution of authority to business and labour which far exceeded the scale and scope of the modest advisory training boards established in most other Canadian jurisdictions. The corporatist model sought to harness the interests of business and labour to forge coherent policies, rationalize programs, and involve generally the private sector in training. The NDP government in the early 1990s expanded the mandate of the agency to include aspects of social policy, eventually enacting the boldest attempt in North America to constitute a corporatist model in labour market policy.

However, business, labour, equity groups, and government were unprepared, unwilling and unable to work together in the nascent agency. The conflict within, and between, the business and labour communities, along with the historical marginalization of the equity groups meant that the board of directors of the agency failed to coalesce as a corporate entity. Furthermore, the leadership of the agency lacked sufficient autonomy from its constituencies and government to make the compromises inherent in designing strategic policy. In 1996, the newly elected Conservative government dissolved the agency and centralized responsibility for labour market adjustment policy in the ministry of education. The liquidation of OTAB was not surprising given that the agency had floundered miserably; however, the wholesale extermination of the corporatist model failed to preserve, and build on, its benefits and accomplishments. As suggested later in this chapter, there are organizational arrangements that avoid both the dysfunction of the OTAB model and the centralization of policy making in government.

The skills development ministry and the training board were severely hampered in their ability to act autonomously, which meant that for the most part they remained paralyzed. Powerful ministries in government confined MSD, while powerful groups in society, as well as politicians and civil servants neutered OTAB. This partly explains why the two agencies fabricated few substantive proposals, and why OTAB was preoccupied with developing convoluted procedures and processes. Unlike organizations that were able to adapt to broader societal values — such as Clark's adult education schools, Selznick's watershed agency, Zald's community agency, and Brint and Karabel's colleges discussed in the first chapter — MSD and OTAB floundered and were extinguished.

The central value that MSD sought to institutionalize, greater reliance on on-the-job training, was precarious because dominant organizations and interests (the colleges and education ministries) opposed the expansion of industrial training. As a result, the department became isolated from, and ignored by, the powerful education ministries and the colleges, eventually becoming less and less able to respond to government demands for coordinated and strategic policy. Without allies in the community to combat opposition from the education ministries, the skills development organization fell short in its efforts to remain independent and to effect change.

OTAB was created, in part, to offset the opposition by the educational institutions to on-the-job training by harnessing the interests of business and labour. However, the agency was hindered in that its central value, cooperation between labour, business, and equity groups, was precarious. The pressures OTAB faced were so diverse — augment training for the employed and unemployed in both the public and private sectors, foster equity, respond to government policies, and cultivate business-labour cooperation — that no possible course of action could achieve them all, or even most of them. An early internal OTAB document stated that

> OTAB's target audience is literally everyone! People who are working, people who've lost their jobs, people who employ other people, people who want to join the workforce for the first time, students, trainers, educators and the list goes on. And then there are groups within these groups. People with disabilities, people from different racial backgrounds, women, francophones, etc. The ... challenge will to reach these audiences and leave them with the impression that OTAB is doing important work that's of potential benefit to

themselves and all Ontarians (OTAB draft communications and marketing plan, August 1993, p. 1).

The challenge proved to be a hopeless one. The lack of consensus about priorities meant that the agency could not chart a path that was acceptable to its powerful stakeholders.

The training agency's key stakeholder, government, provided the agency with insufficient autonomy, expecting it to conform to the norms of a line ministry in staffing and management practices. Business interests, on the other hand, wanted a streamlined agency focused on industrial training; labour favoured an organizational structure modelled after labour federations; while equity groups remained fixated on righting historical inequities. The four-year consultation period, commencing in 1989, as well as the size of the agency caused labour, business, and equity groups to believe their incompatible visions for the agency would be heeded by Cabinet.

Both organizations operated in a capitalist society within which the involvement of the state in the labour market is, itself, precarious. Indeed, beginning in the 1970s the role of the state in general became more precarious as the neo-Conservative economic paradigm, and its acceptance of high unemployment rates and a smaller role for government, gained ascent (Shields and Evans 1998).

Both MSD and OTAB faced high expectations. As newly created organizations, key groups — Cabinet, other ministries, and business, labour and equity groups — anticipated innovative and significant proposals to improve policy and coordination. In OTAB's case, the lengthy birthing process caused expectations for dramatic short-term transformations of policy to reach excessive levels. Not surprisingly, the inability to meet the expectations caused the legitimacy of both organizations to suffer, especially when political power shifted. The unsettled political climate in the province (in the span of 11 years there were five premiers, from three different parties and eight ministers with responsibility for labour market adjustment) spawned additional problems for the two agencies. This atypical period of political instability in Ontario worked against the agencies acting as a chance or random factor that could not be guarded against.

The measurement of outcomes for organizations in institutional environments is, as previously discussed, impracticable or, at the very least, extremely formidable; hence, organizations gain legitimacy by acting in such a way that makes it difficult to determine the extent to which a problem has been corrected. The fact that MSD, and especially OTAB, failed to offer schemes (no matter how rudimentary) to remedy the problems they were created to address is significant in understanding their eventual demise. Institutions such as churches, hospitals, and schools do not necessarily alleviate dysfunctional social conditions, but they are perceived to be engaged in addressing these and providing explanations for the persistence of the problems. At OTAB the disparate views of business and labour precluded even reaching any agreement as to why the agency was failing while the "imperative of maintaining the fragile consensus at the board level led to a lowest common denominator approach to agenda setting" and the dearth of policy innovation (Haddow and Sharpe 1997, p. 272).

With regard to OTAB, several observers have pointed to corporatism as the root cause of the agency's derisory performance and demise (Haddow and Sharpe 1997; Wolfe 1997; Bradford 1998). Then again, the failure of the decidedly non-corporatist skills development ministry in the 1980s suggests that the reasons for OTAB's collapse cannot solely reside in its corporatist structure. The MSD experience showed that issues of training and labour market adjustment reside at the intersection of several powerful, entrenched, bureaucratic entities, namely the ministries of education and labour; and any stand-alone agency (corporatist or not) trying to bridge the bureaucratic gaps was doomed to fail.

Although the nature of the environments of MSD and OTAB dramatically impacted on their activities, the inability of both organizations to successfully meet policy challenges was also partly rooted in the nature of their design and therefore a share of the blame for the organizational failures falls to the designers and operational leaders of the two agencies. The designers failed to provide the organizations with adequate tools for their tasks, strikingly so given the environment of the agencies, but at the same time, the operational leaders of these organizations did not sufficiently attempt to alter the conditions they found themselves in.

By deviating from the Premier's Council model, OTAB was insufficiently buffered by its designers from changes that might occur in its environment and the agency came to be seen as a creature of the NDP. By being closely associated with the previous government, the Conservatives in 1995 were uninterested in salvaging the useful aspects of the agency. Indeed, the manner of the demise of the training board was not normal bureaucratic politics, but it indicates the ideological nature of the decision of the Conservative government in 1996. OTAB's decline was disorderly and managed poorly, reflecting the complete loss of legitimacy, lack of leadership, and low level of institutionalization achieved by the agency.

The history of the two training bodies illustrates what happens when organizations cannot adapt to the values of key groups, fail to find domain consensus, and lose legitimacy. From their inception, the MSD and especially OTAB were flawed because their designers failed to appreciate adequately the institutional environments of their creations. The ministry did not have the capacity to build a grass-roots constituency, while the leadership structure of the training board failed to sufficiently consider the fragmentation of interests within business and labour, and the distrust between labour, business, and government. The saga of the two bureaus demonstrates that in an environment pervaded by precarious values, leaders of new organizations are relatively powerless to alter events. This is not to suggest that leaders are unimportant, only that they have few options for action because they cannot establish a new policy regime by altering the mandate and domains of the organizations.

Nevertheless, leadership is important because it can be altered quickly unlike other organizational variables such as design, culture, and size. An environment of precarious values can allow for strong leaders to emerge seeking to build new arrangements and coalitions while increasing the prestige and legitimacy of an organization. In fact, leadership is "a highly contingent situational variable, and the match of leader to situation must be precise" (Brown 1997, p. 67).

In MSD's case, different leadership could have allowed the ministry to operate more effectively by building coalitions with other ministries and the colleges; however, no matter how effective the leadership, MSD could not have coordinated labour market adjustment policy to the extent required to bring about strategic initiatives. Even highly effective leadership could not have overcome the long-standing competition between industrial and institutional training, nor built strong linkages with business and labour. In OTAB's case, different leadership could have prevented some of the bitterness that arose between groups and possibly avoided the complete collapse and dissolution of the agency.

Public agencies in institutional environments, that is with multiple constituencies and with outputs that elude measurement, have difficulty in performing effectively. This is because policymakers are blocked from making changes by the power of the constituents or clients, including their ability to appeal to "ill-defined values and commitments" (Meyer and Zucker 1989, p. 112). The MSD and OTAB experience provides support for this perspective in that OTAB, with its greater stakeholder involvement, did perform more poorly than MSD.

The corporatist model of OTAB was partly an effort to reduce the "use of governmental organizational resources to realize policy goals," in other words, to privatize policy development (Howlett and Ramesh 1993, p. 19). The agency represented an attempt to deal with the ill-defined objectives and divergent interests in the policy field by imposing private-sector values and incentives to enhance effectiveness. Its history demonstrates that the state is unable to grant legitimacy, even through the use of extensive public consultation and legislation, to organizations in an environment of precarious values. As such, the death of the agency suggests that it is too simplistic to assume that the inclusion of stakeholders will improve longevity or performance.

The birth, life, and death of MSD and OTAB illustrate the difficulty of organizations in environments characterized by precarious values: if societal values are precarious it is, *de facto*, impossible to arrange for self-reproducing behaviours that are necessary for institutionalization. The organizations that triumph under such conditions will tend to be small in size, limited in mandate, and have humble expectations associated with them, in order to withstand environmental turmoil, and to minimize the expectations and demands from major stakeholders. Certain organizational characteristics, "smallness, low visibility, secretiveness ... and technological complexity," can protect organizations threatened by termination (Frantz 1992, p. 181).

The training agency experiments in Ontario elucidate the limits of what organizations can accomplish and raise the question as to whether policy development and coordination can be attained without resorting to new organizations. A strong policy vision and commitment to implementation from political leaders can result in effective policy without elaborate new organizational structures, a situation that existed under the Conservatives in the 1970s and early 1980s when Bill Davis was premier. Such an approach is dependent on one or more individuals who are knowledgeable and invest political capital, but ultimately power will shift and with it the policy direction, as occurred in 1985 when Davis resigned. Because training is "a 'valence' political issues, in which partisan conflict is about the most effective means to the achievement of an agreed upon end" relying solely on individual leadership is problematic (Evans 1992, p. viii). Organizations are indispensable because they are deliberately designed to "institutionalize services deemed necessary, services whose demands are ... to outlast a single sponsor or bureaucrat" (deLeon 1978, p. 288). Only organizational, if not institutional, foundations can provide some protection from the turmoil in this policy field. As discussed below, there are organizational models that can begin to provide a stronger substructure to training policy.

Labour market adjustment, to be effective, requires involvement from groups outside government; politicians acting alone will fail to provide adequate long-term leadership. State action alone, no matter how well designed, cannot generate effective labour market adjustment policy, nor spawn a training culture, because by definition the outcomes of training must meet labour market conditions. One approach is for the state to withdraw altogether, but this has not been done by even the most conservative political parties given the rate of technological change and the adjustment challenges faced by unemployed (and employed) workers. At the other extreme are corporatist approaches, which can outlast individuals, that directly couple the state with business and labour.

Canada has been ranked near or at the bottom in international comparisons on corporatism and centralization (Dell'Aringa and Lodovici 1992). This hints that there is an opportunity in Canada to move toward policy mechanisms that have some (greater) degree of corporatism. However, corporatism as a political strategy has been under pressure in the 1980s and 1990s even in countries ranked high vis-à-vis corporatism and centralization: Austria, Sweden, Japan, and Germany. The key factors in undermining corporatist practices have been the decline of national markets, technological innovation, and the fragmentation of labour markets (Treu 1992, pp. 4-5). Thus, corporatist structures in Canada are likely to face significant initial barriers and ongoing challenges.

## LESSONS

What can be learned about labour market adjustment policy from the lives of MSD and OTAB? The failure of the organizations charged with labour market adjustment policy does not imply that government has withdrawn from this area, for organizational death did not mean large-scale policy termination. Although the MSD and OTAB structures were disbanded, there was no fundamental change to policy or program capacity, even if policies were somewhat less effective since institutional training remained dominant and private-sector groups were excluded from decision making. Labour market adjustment policy in Ontario will increase in political priority during the next decade for at least four reasons, each providing some stimulus for the participation of business and labour in training policy.

First, technological change will continue at a rapid rate and international competition will not abate; and therefore Ontario, as the manufacturing heartland of Canada, will remain under pressure to ensure that its workforce is competitive. Given the nature of the North American labour market, businesses will continue to under-invest in training, and look to government to furnish a trained workforce. Indeed, since World War II the state has provided a range of supports to economic growth to ensure that business has the latest technology and the most highly trained workforce (O'Connor 1973). In past decades, institutional training received by young people often sufficed for the remainder of their careers; this is becoming less and less the case, necessitating state intervention for laid-off workers and others.

Second, from the late 1980s there has been a general decrease in government program expenditures (in constant dollars), including those for labour market adjustment. When expenditures are decreasing, there is little advantage for governments, or indeed for business and labour, to participate in corporatist-like arrangements. Labour and business might reach agreement on how to spend additional funds, but they are unlikely to consent, as illustrated by the OTAB experience, to elimination of services for their constituencies. Thus, it is best for governments to retain and centralize authority to avoid lengthy discussion over, and opposition to, funding reductions. This, of course, was the strategy adopted by the Conservatives in 1996 when OTAB was disbanded. As government expenditures begin to recover, policy making will become more flexible and the involvement of external groups will become less acrimonious, and hence more suitable and necessary.

Third, when Ontario assumes authority for federal programs, total provincial expenditures on labour market adjustment will more than double since half a billion dollars of previously federal funding will now be under provincial care. The 1996 federal proposal to transfer responsibilities to the provinces suggested that labour and business should play a central role in policy, including the assessment and evaluation of programs. The expansion of provincial jurisdiction to incorporate the training and related needs of (un)employment insurance recipients has required the creation of a new administrative and policy infrastructure. In June 1999, after the Conservative government's re-election, a new ministry was announced by the premier. The Ministry of Training, Colleges and Universities re-creates the pre-1985 arrangement of one organization accountable for both postsecondary institutional and industrial training.

Fourth, during the second half of the 1990s unemployment rates have decreased so that labour market adjustment has not been a political or policy priority other than, to some extent, in the area of youth. However, unemployment rates will increase again when North American economies enter (as they must) the next recession, which will turn the stoplight again onto active labour market policies. Ontario, along with some other provinces, will be especially liable under such conditions as training and related programs will be solely under provincial authority. As such, decisionmakers may well turn to business and labour to assist in the formulation of well-informed and balanced policies.

In summary, notwithstanding the failure of MSD and OTAB, there will be continued pressure for the participation of business and labour in labour market adjustment policy. International competition, rising government expenditures, and federal devolution can be expected to elicit new organizational arrangements. At the same time, labour market adjustment policy will remain a field imbued with precarious values and therefore difficult to coordinate.

## RECOMMENDATIONS

The failure of the MSD and OTAB should not be perceived as dysfunctional and solely a misallocation of resources. To some degree the agencies can be considered a success in that the demise displays the organizational arrangements which are ineffective in labour market adjustment policy. The failures are an opportunity to learn and apply this knowledge in designing more robust and effective bureaus and policies. As one observer and decisionmaker in this field has noted, "If some of the experiments undertaken to date prove to be false starts, then serious thought will need to be given to what might work better in the Canadian environment" (Kroeger 1995, p. 235).

What, therefore, is an effective organizational model for coordinating labour market policy in Ontario? Effective arrangements are based on an in-depth and historical understanding of the policy field, including past failures, a knowledge of organizational capacities, and moderate expectations. The model described below avoids the two extremes of centralizing policy responsibility in government (either in a stand-alone training ministry or within a larger education ministry) and devolving it entirely to the private sphere.

The model recognizes that the fragmentation of business and labour interests in North America means that it is a formidable task "to centralize or coordinate training expenditures above the microlevel" (Wever 1995, p. 113). The model takes as a given that until societal values change and institutional structures become possible, the state is the only actor able to make policy and funding decisions, in other words, policy-making corporatist structures are not possible if values are precarious. Lastly, the model recognizes that making training a less precarious value, that is, to foster more agreement by major groups, insulate organizations from changes in power relationships, and foster a training culture, requires an incremental methodology.

The OTAB experience shows that business and labour share insufficient common objectives or values to develop policy, while the MSD history suggests that the state acting alone cannot shift training toward less precarious values and effective policy. Therefore, the model proposed below rests on the premise that an effective organization for training policy must initially be imposed by the state. The premise is in opposition to the notion that over time the invisible hand of self-interest will cause corporatist institutions to arise (Hayek 1973).

The model, which builds on some of the ideas proposed by the Premier's Council in 1990, has two components: first, an advisory committee on labour market policy composed of the labour, business, and government elite. Such a body has been proposed before in Ontario, for example, in 1985 when MSD was created, and existed in the form of the Premier's Council in 1989-90 and also exists in several provinces. The members of the advisory council would be selected by government with a mandate to provide advice on strategic labour market policy. Only leaders from those sectors interested in participating would be appointed by government, which likely would include larger corporations and private-sector unions, primarily the manufacturing and high technology sectors. In any case, it would be critical to ensure that the stature of the individuals selected is high, especially within their own communities. The advisory committee would report to the minister responsible for training policy who would also be a member of the committee. Business and labour would be required to make a modest financial contribution to the cost of operating the advisory committee, perhaps seconding staff to the committee's secretariat, which itself would be small and staffed primarily by civil servants with a sprinkling of academics and others.

Unlike the large OTAB board of directors, the membership of this body must be small, no more than 15 individuals, to force business and labour representatives to have broad visions and facilitate decision making. Membership in this body would be especially appealing to labour and business groups in Ontario since the transfer of federal funds means that the province will largely determine how employment insurance monies for training, which are contributed solely by employers and workers, are spent.

The second component of the model is an operational agency for the delivery of workplace training programs, including apprenticeship and other industrial training services. This agency would have responsibility for delivering state-funded training programs but *not* for allocating resources or making policy. Such an agency would have a leadership structure closely resembling that of other arm's-length operational agencies with a board of directors appointed by government and composed primarily of key stakeholders. The members and chair — all highly knowledgeable in program delivery — would be appointed by government based partly on the advice from the labour market advisory committee. The board of directors would be relatively small (no more than 15 members) without representation from equity groups, while the agency's staff, unlike OTAB's, would not remain civil servants to ensure the necessary degree of flexibility to deliver programs. The agency's probability of success will be aided by the shift of power toward industrial training, and away from institutional training, which will occur within the Ministry of Training, Colleges and Universities when federal funding devolves to the province.

There are relatively few risks to government associated with this model, indeed, the new structures might have an innate appeal to politicians as a symbol of a new direction for labour market policy necessitated by the conditions discussed previously, particularly the federal devolution. The advisory body can always be ignored if its advice proves fractured or incoherent, as is the case with all advisory bodies, thus decreasing the risks of failure for the government. In any case, policy advice from the advisory body would be filtered and augmented by Cabinet. At the same time, if policies ultimately prove ineffective some of the blame can be allocated to the advisory body, thus insulating politicians somewhat from the unpredictability of labour market conditions. The experience of the Premier's Council, and other jurisdictions, suggests that key stakeholders, in fact, are able to develop, and agree on, broad visionary directions.

The operational agency would be concerned solely with efficient and effective service delivery, having no role in designing policies and programs, setting funding levels and evaluation. During its brief life OTAB confirmed that programs are delivered as effectively, if not more so, by an arm's-length agency than by a government ministry. The members on the board of this agency would be selected for their operational knowledge of programs and charged with ensuring that programs work as well as possible.

The operational agency would, initially, have responsibility for apprenticeship and other on-the-job training programs (along with some of the federal programs transferred to the province), representing approximately $200 million in expenditures. The relatively small budget avoids, or at least minimizes, a dilemma faced by OTAB: large budgets beget a high level of accountability.

The model allows business and labour to work on visionary and operational issues, but not policy and funding, recognizing the "hyper-pluralist" nature of Canadian polity and labour market policy in particular (Sharpe and Haddow 1997, p. 20). Over time the middle ground, policy making, initially occupied solely by government might be unbolted to allow for larger roles for business and labour. The organizational model is not unlike that utilized in other areas: health care, education, and culture in which services are funded largely by government, which retains power to make policy based on advice from stakeholders, yet delivered by agencies (hospitals, public housing agencies, colleges and universities, museums, and art galleries) with boards of directors appointed solely or primarily by government. If the operational agency performs well then some proportion of the directors could be appointed by the stakeholders, as occurs in some areas (universities and hospitals), but not others (public housing agencies).

What has been most precarious with respect to labour market adjustment is the middle ground between broad strategic policy and program delivery. These decisions — funding levels, policies, and programs in response to socio-economic conditions, and the degree of emphasis on equity — must remain within government. Politicians and bureaucrats are unwilling to privatize these, while at the same time business and labour are unable to agree on these issues. As the OTAB saga showed, business and labour are insufficiently organized internally to have coherent policy positions, and certainly are unable to make policy trade-offs. Further, the OTAB experience also emphasizes that any devolution of policy making to business and labour breeds alarm and anxiety among politicians and bureaucrats. In short, an organizational structure that requires business and labour to make policy, and prevents politicians from doing so, is doomed to fail.

Expectations must be kept to a minimum, especially on the part of politicians. "There is a tendency to embark upon a policy initiative with all trumpets blaring and to claim to produce 'the' solution to the problem" (Hogwood and Peters 1982, p. 243). This creates cynicism on the part of clients and stakeholders, and indeed, overcoming the distaste left by the OTAB ordeal among business and labour will be a challenge in implementing a new model. Furthermore, by proclaiming "the" solution, organizations and policies are made too rigid, leaving later improvements or alterations difficult to bring about.

The model is not without dangers and all parties must, from the beginning, recognize these. The policy-operations schism evident in MSD will re-emerge to some extent, but can be minimized by requiring formal and informal mechanisms, such as secondments, physical proximity, and joint projects, to be instituted to ensure that the gap between the operational agency and the policy staff in government does not become dysfunctional. The creation of two new bodies, no matter that they are relatively small, will be perceived by some stakeholders as unnecessary or more trouble than they are worth, especially by the colleges. However, if related to the transfer of federal program responsibility to the province, their genesis would be a logical innovation.

Class and power hostility will arise in the two agencies, and again steps must be taken to minimize it, such as discouraging the emergence of a corporate culture that favours caucuses and narrow self-interest. Government must make it explicit from the beginning that individual members are not representing constituencies. Moulding an *esprit de corps* will be facilitated because the members will be selected by government with an eye toward those most adept at the social bargaining that will be required. The presence of Cabinet ministers, and their mediation skills, on the advisory body should also aid in avoiding some of the infighting prevalent at OTAB.

Finally, decisionmakers need to be cognizant of the precarious values in crafting policy and organizations in labour market adjustment policy. The fragmented nature of the policy field and its satiation with precarious values means that it is a harsh environment for organizations to operate, and for policies to succeed, within. This calls for attention to several of the lessons discussed in Chapters 3 and 4. In particular, vigilance must be used to avoid expanding the mandate of any new agency as occurred with MSD when its mission grew to encompass literacy and laid-off workers in 1987, and with OTAB when it was given jurisdiction for labour market entry and equity concerns. In both cases the expansion of organizational domains raised expectations, weakened the agencies, and proved to be dysfunctional.

In summary, more planning and consideration of environmental conditions, inside and outside government, will increase the likelihood of organizational success. At the same time, matters of policy and organization in labour market policy do not lend themselves easily to ideal solutions. There are no guarantees, but there are methods that can make the odds of organizational survival and ultimate institutionalization more favourable.

# APPENDIX A

# Dramatis Personae

The first part the Appendix is a description of the key actors in the Ministry of Skills Development and the Ontario Training and Adjustment Board drama, including the background of members of the OTAB board of directors. The second part summarizes the key dates and events from 1985 to 1996, together with a listing of all the training agency's board of director meetings.

## ORGANIZATIONAL LEADERS

Organizations are particular arrangements of individuals and technologies. Some individuals, by virtue of the authority and power they can have, are more important in accounting for organizational events than other actors. Listed below are key organizational leaders of the events studied, all but seven were interviewed.

## 1985-1990

*Politicians*

| | |
|---|---|
| William Davis | Premier 1971-85. |
| Frank Miller | Premier 1985. |
| David Peterson | Premier 1985-90. |

| | |
|---|---|
| Ernie Eves | Minister of MSD 1985. |
| Phil Gillies | Minister of MSD 1985. |
| Gregory Sorbara | Minister of MSD 1985-87. |
| Alvin Curling | Minister of MSD 1987-89. |
| Sean Conway | Minister of MSD, MoEd, and MCU 1989-90. |

*Civil Servants*

| | |
|---|---|
| Blair Tully | Deputy minister of MSD 1985-87. |
| Glenna Carr | Deputy minister of MSD 1987-89. |
| Bernard Shapiro | Deputy minister of MoEd 1986-1990, acting deputy minister of MSD 1989-90, associate secretary of Cabinet 1990. |
| Les Horswill | Assistant deputy minister (policy) of MSD 1985-92. |

**1990-1996**

*Politicians*

| | |
|---|---|
| Robert Rae | Premier 1990-95. |
| Richard Allen | Minister of MSD, MCU and OTAB Secretariat 1990-93. |
| Dave Cooke | Minister of MET, responsible for OTAB 1993-95. |
| Michael Harris | Premier 1995- |
| John Snobelen | Minister of MET, responsible for OTAB 1995-97. |

*Civil Servants*

| | |
|---|---|
| David Wolfe | Executive coordinator of Cabinet Committee on Economic and Labour Policy 1990-93. |
| Naomi Alboim | Deputy minister of OTAB Secretariat 1991-93. |
| Charles Pascal | Deputy minister of MET 1993-95. |
| Timothy Millard | Interim chief executive officer of OTAB 1993-94. |
| Garth Jackson | Chief executive officer of OTAB 1994-96. |

## Members of OTAB Board of Directors

| | |
|---|---|
| Donald Green | Co-chair (business) of OTAB. |
| Glenn Pattinson | Co-chair (labour) of OTAB. |
| John Howatson | Associate co-chair (business) of OTAB.[1] |
| Erna Post | Associate co-chair (labour) of OTAB.[1] |

Listed below are the members of the OTAB board of directors, their affiliations, and a brief description of their occupations. Fifteen of these individuals were interviewed.

### Business

| | |
|---|---|
| Allen Berg | Small business owner. |
| Vance Curry | Mid-level manager in large firm. (Resigned in 1994.) |
| Bill Dover | Consultant. (Replaced Vance Curry.) |
| Donald Green (co-chair) | Owner of mid-sized auto parts company. |
| Marilyn Jones | Mid-level manager for large company. |
| Peter Lo | Owner of auto parts company. |
| Dace Phillips | Mid-level manager for large corporation. |
| Pauline Sauvé | Owner of small consulting firm. |
| Roland Turner | Small business owner. |

### Labour

| | |
|---|---|
| Patrick Dillon | Elected union leader. |
| Maxine Jones | English instructor at a community college. |
| Sue Milling | Researcher for steelworkers union. |
| Jay Nair | Coordinator of education-related issues. |
| Glenn Pattinson (co-chair) | Union vice-president. |
| Elizabeth Plettenberg | Retired union staff member. (Resigned in 1994.)[2] |
| Michael Reilly | Retired union leader. (Replaced George Ward.) |

| David Robertson | Union staff officer. |
| George Ward | Union advisor. (Resigned in 1994.) |

## Equity Groups

| Stan Delaney (persons with disabilities) | Staff of advocacy agency. |
| Michelle Labelle (francophones) | School principal. |
| Annamaria Menozzi (women) | Consultant. |
| Karanja Njoroge (racial minorities) | University administrator. (Resigned in 1994.) |
| Ratna Omidvar | Executive director of community agency. (Replaced Karanja Njoroge.) |
| Scott Seiler (alternate director for persons with disabilities) | Consultant. |

## Education/Training

| Jane Dobell | Retired school trustee. (Replaced Teresa González.) |
| Teresa González | School administrator. (Resigned in 1994.) |
| Mark Waldron | University professor. |

## Government (ex-officio)

| Joan Andrew (Ontario) | Assistant deputy minister at MET. |
| Bonnie Ewart (municipal) | Commissioner of social services. |
| Julyan Reid (federal) | Executive director of federal department. |

## *Associate Co-Chairs*[1]

John Howatson          Associate co-chair (business) of OTAB.
Erna Post                    Associate co-chair (labour) of OTAB.


Notes

[1]The associate co-chairs of OTAB were not members of the board of directors, but were selected by business and labour.
[2]The OFL did not replace Plettenberg, thus reducing the number of labour directors to seven after 1994.


## CHRONOLOGY

The chronology enumerates the key events of the organizational and policy sagas of MSD and OTAB.


## 1985

| | |
|---|---|
| March 22 | Miller announces establishment of MSD. |
| March 25 | Order-in-Council signed for MSD; election called. |
| May | No party gains sufficient seats to form majority government. |
| June | Federal government announces the Canadian Jobs Strategy. |
| June 11 | Bill 9 introduced by Conservatives to formalize mandate of MSD. |
| June 26 | Liberals form minority government with NDP; Sorbara appointed minister of MCU. |
| October | Creation of MSD approved, with Sorbara as minister; FUTURES program for youth introduced by MSD. |

## 1986

April        Bill 9 reintroduced by Liberals to formalize mandate of MSD.

June         Ontario training strategy for adults introduced by MSD.

## 1987

Spring       MSD gains approval for Help Centres and Transition program.

Summer       Election; Liberals form majority government.

Fall         Curling is named minister of MSD; literacy policy transferred to MSD.

## 1988

             Attempts to design and coordinate labour market adjustment policies.

## 1989

January      Premier's Council begins to study training and education policy.

April        Federal government announces Labour Force Development Strategy.

August       Conway appointed minister of MSD, MoEd, and MCU; Cabinet Committee on Education, Training and Adjustment created.

September    Shapiro appointed acting deputy minister of MSD.

Fall         Cabinet decides to curtail MSD and decentralize programs (implemented in early 1990).

## 1990

Summer      Election called, won by NDP.

July        Premier's Council report released.

October     NDP Cabinet announced; Allen appointed minister of MSD and MCU.

## 1991

May         Cabinet approves the creation of OTAB.

Summer      OTAB Secretariat formed to guide creation of OTAB.

November    Allen publicly announces OTAB to be established.

December    Federal government announces the establishment of the CLFDB.

## 1992

Fall        Jobs Ontario Training program announced.

November    Bill 96 (to establish OTAB) introduced in the Legislature.

## 1993

Spring      Amalgamation of MCU, MSD, MoEd, OTAB Project, and Jobs Ontario Training program to create MET.

July        Bill 96 receives third reading and Royal assent; OTAB board of directors appointed.

September   First board meeting; MSD ceases to exist.

October     Strategic planning session by the board of directors.

## 1994

Summer      First public meeting of OTAB; Jackson hired as permanent chief executive officer of OTAB.

December    Second public meeting.

## 1995

February    First meetings of the OTAB councils to review programs.

Spring      Election called (won by the Conservatives).

Summer      Snobelen appointed minister, institutes review of training policy.

## 1996

January     OTAB board meeting boycotted by business board members.

April       Government announces that OTAB is to be dissolved.

May         Federal government proposes transfer of training program responsibilities to the provinces.

## Dates for the 14 meetings of the OTAB board of directors.

1993        21-22 September, 26-27 October, 16-17 November, 14-15 December.

1994        22-23 February, 26-27 April, 16 June, 9 August, 18-19 October, 13 December.

1995        5 April, 6 June, 19 September, 3-4 October.

1996        The meeting scheduled for January 1996 was boycotted by the business board members.

# APPENDIX B

# Methodology

The creation and death of public-sector organizations and the policy produced and implemented by these agencies is difficult to study because key decisions are made behind closed doors. There is little opportunity for researchers to observe and obtain data on the internal-to-government processes that ultimately result in decisions about organizational life and death. David Good asks:

> How ... can a researcher expect to get answers to his [sic] questions? Parliamentary government ... is inextricably tied to the fundamentals of cabinet solidarity and ministerial responsibility. Information flows through private circuits — personal telephone conversations, confidential memoranda, closely guarded briefing notes, or selective dinner parties. Decisions are taken in private — over intimate lunch-time chats, in the sanctity of a department office, or behind the closed doors of a cabinet committee room. Civil servants are, quite understandably, sworn to their oaths of secrecy, politicians maintain their mutually accepted pledges of confidentiality to their fellow colleagues, and outsiders, the few who have links to the inside, protect their sources to maintain their access (1980, p. 199).

This book is built on three sources: documents, interviews, and participant observation. Each of these is reviewed below, along with suggestions for conducting research on public policy.

The *documents* relied upon for the autopsy of MSD and OTAB fall into three categories. The first are government documents produced for public dissemination: *Hansard*, press releases, consultation papers, speeches, the public accounts, etc. The second group of documents — Cabinet submissions, briefing notes, internal studies and evaluations, memoranda, etc. — is not in the public domain. Third are the documents produced by groups external to government, such as the OTAB reference groups.

There are two major problems associated with using government documents: (i) locating appropriate source(s) of data and (ii) obtaining the data from government agencies (Klassen and LeBlanc 1993*a*). Most government departments regularly produce their own data in press releases, papers, studies, and annual reports that they maintain in their own files. Public access to these data is usually via departmental libraries or information centres, which means dealing with numerous decentralized information sources. Few agencies provide master lists of their published data. Some centralized sources of data exist beyond departmental libraries, such as university libraries acting as "depositories" for government documents. However, despite the considerable information to be found in such central depositories, their collections do not encompass the depth and breadth of information necessitated for detailed analysis.

Archives, such as the Archives of Ontario, provide a potentially vast centralized repository for government documents. However, typically their collections are of material at least five, if not ten years, of age. Furthermore, in Ontario, many documents cannot be released until 20 years have elapsed since their creation. These constraints severely limit the utility of archives in providing data necessary to understand recent, or even relatively recent, events.

Once relevant available data have been identified, the next step is to obtain it from government departments. A number of circumstances complicate this seemingly simple step. For example, data may not be organized to allow easy retrieval, it may not be available in the format that is required for research purposes, and financial costs may be substantial for data retrieval. Typically, the more legitimate a request is deemed (from the perspective of government officials), the more likely the researcher is to get assistance from government personnel.

This study was limited by the fact that some data which could have been useful for the analysis were not available for research purposes. Generally, because the events surrounding MSD lay further in the past it was easier to obtain documents than for more recent events around OTAB. Documents related to the dissolution of OTAB were most difficult to obtain because of the recency of events. The researcher's status as an "insider" did enable him informally to gain access to some of the confidential documents.

*Interviews* with key decisionmakers and observers comprise the second component of the database for this book. The objective of the interview methodology was to obtain data (motivations, beliefs, etc.) that was not recorded in formal documents, as well as to shed light on events for which documents could not be accessed (Klassen and LeBlanc 1993*b*).

Interviews were conducted with 78 individuals, including premiers, ministers, deputy ministers, OTAB board members, and others inside and outside the provincial government. Seventeen persons were interviewed more than once, in order to obtain additional data or to seek clarification on data already collected. In total, 98 separate interviews were conducted (three were over the telephone and two through written correspondence) comprising more than 180 hours. The position held and principal organizational affiliation of those interviewed is shown in Tables A1 and A2.

Two premiers, two Cabinet ministers, four deputies, and two OTAB board members refused to be interviewed, resulting in an interview response rate of 89 percent. Of the ten individuals who declined to be interviewed only two held positions central to the events under analysis: Glenna Carr, deputy minister of MSD from 1987 to 1989, and Bob Rae, premier from 1990 to 1995. However, interviews with other key participants were able to elicit some of the data that Carr and Rae might have provided.

Approximately half of the interviews were conducted using a prepared interview schedule. For all interviews, hand-written notes were taken during the interview, and in most cases these were returned to the interviewee for review. In about 35 percent of interviews the interviewees requested changes to the interview notes, usually minor, but in some cases significant new information was provided by interviewees.

The decision to not use a tape recorder was motivated by a desire to maximize the degree of candour and openness of those interviewed. Furthermore, the interviews sought primarily to determine the motivations and attitudes of participants, rather than to re-create sequences of events.

Based on interviews for this book, five methodological suggestions have been developed for interviews with government policymakers and organizational leaders. These are outlined beginning on page 175.

**Table A1: Principal Position, During 1985 to 1996, of Persons Interviewed**

|  | n | % |
|---|---|---|
| Premier | 2 | 3 |
| Minister | 5 | 6 |
| Deputy minister | 9 | 11 |
| OTAB board member[1] | 15 | 19 |
| Assistant deputy minister | 14 | 18 |
| Director or manager | 16 | 20 |
| Professional staff | 9 | 11 |
| Other[2] | 8 | 10 |
| Total | 78 | 99 (rounding) |

Notes: [1]Includes the two associate co-chairs of OTAB.
[2]Persons in this category included members of Opposition parties, the federal government, union officials, and academics.

**Table A2: Principal Organizational Affiliation, During 1985 to 1996, of Persons Interviewed**

|  | n | % |
|---|---|---|
| Elected member of the Legislature | 8 | 10 |
| Ministry of Skills Development/OTAB | 25 | 32 |
| OTAB board of directors[1] | 15 | 19 |
| Other ministries | 15 | 19 |
| Central agencies | 9 | 11 |
| Non-provincial government | 6 | 8 |
| Total | 78 | 99 (rounding) |

Note: [1]Includes the two associate co-chairs of OTAB.

**Key Informant.** A key supporter or informant can play a major role in making an interview methodology a successful one. The value of a key informant is two-fold. First, he or she can provide "insider" information during the formulation of the research design. For example, the key supporter can provide an initial list of people to be interviewed. Second, this individual can be used to leverage involvement from other individuals who may otherwise decline to participate in the study. In the research related to MSD, a deputy minister was a key informant thereby creating a higher level of comfort than would otherwise have existed on the part of his colleagues when they were interviewed.

Concomitant with the benefits presented above, a key informant will also introduce negative consequences to the research process. For example, the informant may be perceived, by some, to have biased the research process to ensure that the findings ultimately support whatever ideological or policy position(s) the key informant holds. In other words, the researcher's objectivity may be called into question if he/she is viewed as being too closely associated with the informant.

**Timing.** The decision as to when to conduct interviews during the research process demands careful consideration. The general rule in the literature is that interviews "are more fruitful when some knowledge of variables is already available" (Walizer and Wienir 1978, p. 266). By conducting interviews after a review of documents, the focus of the interviews rests less on the gathering of basic data and more on the informal and non-documented social processes, such as attitudes and motivations.

The order in which individuals are to be interviewed needs careful consideration in the research design. The strategy adopted for this book, based on suggestions by Heclo and Wildavsky (1974), was to conduct interviews first with persons who had retired from government. Compared to other groups, these persons were more open to answering questions with candour and had more time available. The next group of persons interviewed were those who, while still with government, were now employed in other agencies or positions than those under study. The next group included lower-ranking officials, followed by middle-managers and last by the most senior leaders such as premiers, ministers, and agency chairs.

**Access.** Gaining access to decisionmakers represents a challenge to many researchers who use interviews. The strategy employed for this study was to treat the interview no differently from any other meeting that the interviewee might attend. The assumption was that the more typical of organizational practices and procedures the initial contact, the more likely it would be that it would elicit a positive reply.

A personalized letter on university letterhead was sent to those persons identified for interviews. The letter explained how his or her current or past position made them significant informants and/or observer of the matter under study, and it asked for a meeting. A telephone call was made a few days later to confirm arrangements and, if requested, a set of questions to be discussed was forwarded. In some cases the researcher was also asked to provide a list of other persons to be interviewed.

If telephone contact proved unsuccessful in obtaining an interview, the researcher would appear (unannounced) at the office of the prospective interviewee to request a meeting time. It proved more difficult — although not impossible — for gate-keepers to say "no" when the researcher stood in front of them waiting to book an appointment, rather than just being a voice over the telephone. This strategy, however, was not foolproof, for in one case the researcher approached an individual's office on seven separate occasions over a six-month span, and each time was unable to schedule an appointment, although the executive assistant continued to reassure him that an interest remained in arranging an interview.

**Confidentiality,** a general issue of concern in interview research, assumes a prominent role when the events being studied are recent ones. This is especially so when, as in the case of MSD and OTAB, there is significant sensitivity on the part of individuals whose careers and lives have been, or might yet be, impacted by the events under study.

Individuals in middle management were more likely to request additional assurance(s) that their comments would be treated in a confidential manner than more senior or more junior officials. It is hypothesized that those below the middle-management level are protected by collective bargaining agreements and therefore do not fear that their comments to researchers in the interviews will have a negative impact on their careers.

Those individuals at the senior bureaucratic level, as well as politicians, are likely accustomed to fielding interview questions and are knowledgeable about what to say and/or not to say. In fact, several people in very senior positions stated that there was no need for their comments to be treated as confidential. This suggests that the confidentiality needs of groups vary and that precautions should be taken in this regard in the research design.

**Social Processes.** Interviews are a type of interpersonal communication relationship between two people. During most interviews it became obvious that those being interviewed expected a return of information for their provision of information to the interviewer.

The information that the researcher was most frequently asked for were the views and opinions of those persons already interviewed and the conclusions reached by the researcher. The latter type of question was addressed by explaining that it was too early to draw conclusions, but that the researcher would be pleased to mail a summary of findings to the interviewee at the completion of the study (which was done). At times, however, it was possible, and indeed valuable, for the researcher to share some information during the interview process. This was done with general statements, such as "others have presented the point of view that..." which did not violate the confidentiality of the research process. The interest in information from the researcher by many of those interviewed is not surprising given that individuals in leadership positions are often collecting, massaging, and disseminating information.

The final data-collection method was *participant observation.* From 1986-96 the researcher was a policy adviser in the Ontario public service: at the Ministry of Colleges and Universities, the Ministry of Community and Social Services, and at the Treasury and Management boards. His positions within the machinery of government allowed him to utilize both the "insider" and the "outsider" perspectives (Merton 1972). As previously mentioned, the researcher's status as an insider meant that he was able informally to obtain access to documents unavailable to outsiders. His status increased the likelihood of government officials agreeing to be interviewed. As an insider he presented less of a risk to those in government, and their organizations, which encouraged them to speak more openly than would have been the case with an outside researcher. It is doubtful that this book could have been written without the researcher's status as an insider.

In addition to the positive aspects of the researcher's dual status, there were also negative consequences. His insider status at times raised questions about his ability to remain objective and impartial in the minds of those whose cooperation he requested. Lastly, the researcher's selection of MSD and OTAB, rather than other agencies, seemed at times to raise the anxiety level of persons being interviewed. For example, a secretary of Cabinet more than once suggested selecting a more "successful" organization for study.[1]

---

[1] Baum presents some interesting arguments for why organizational researchers choose particular research projects. His main thesis is that "researchers choose fields for study both because they appeal to conscious theoretical interests and because they respond to unconscious conflicts" (Baum 1994, p.138).

# Bibliography

Advisory Council on Adjustment (Jean de Grandpré, Chair). 1989. *Adjusting to Win*. Ottawa: Supply and Services Canada.

Liberals and NDP. 1985. *Agenda for Reform: Proposal for Minority Parliament*. Toronto. 28 May.

Ainslie, Kimble F., ed. 1993. *Conservative Corrections: Democratic Conservatism from the Roots Up*. London (Canada): Springbank Publications.

Aldrich, Howard E. and Jeffrey Pfeffer. 1976. "Environments of Organizations," *Annual Review of Sociology*, 2:79-105.

Argyle, Michael. 1991. *Cooperation: The Basis of Sociability*. London: Routledge.

Aucoin, Peter. 1975. "Pressure Groups and Recent Changes in the Policy-Making Process," in *Pressure Group Behaviour in Canadian Politics*, ed. Paul A. Pross. Toronto: McGraw-Hill Ryerson, pp. 174-92.

Aucoin, Peter and Herman Bakvis. 1988. *The Centralization-Decentralization Conundrum: Organization and Management in the Canadian Government*. Halifax: Institute for Research on Public Policy.

Aucoin, Peter and Richard French. 1974. *Knowledge, Power and Public Policy*. Ottawa: Science Council of Canada.

Bakvis, Herman. 1996. "Federalism, the New Public Management, and Labour Market Development," in *Canada: The State of the Federation 1996*, ed. D. Brown and P. Fafard. Kingston: Institute of Intergovernmental Relations, Queen's University, pp. 135-65.

Baum, Howell S. 1994. "Transference in Organizational Research," *Administration and Society*, 26(2):135-57.

Baum, J. and C. Oliver. 1991. "Institutional Linkages and Organizational Mortality," *Administrative Science Quarterly*, 16:187-218.

Beaujot, Roderic. 1991. *Population Change in Canada: The Challenges of Policy Adaptation*. Toronto: McClelland & Stewart.

Beggs, H.T. 1985. *A Future Course for Apprenticeship and Industrial Training in Ontario, 1985-1989.* Internal document prepared by Skills Development Division, Ministry of Colleges and Universities.

Bell, George G. and Andrew D. Pascoe. 1988. *The Ontario Government: Structure and Functions.* Toronto: Wall & Thompson.

Benson, Kenneth J. 1977*a*. "Innovation and Crisis in Organizational Analysis," *The Sociological Quarterly*, 18 (Winter):3-16.

——.1977*b*. "Organizations: A Dialectical View," *Administrative Science Quarterly*, 22 (March):1-21.

Benson, Ralph. 1985. *Memorandum re: Organization of the Skills Development Division*, 8 February.

Bernstein, Andrew and Michael J. Trebilcock. 1996. *Labour Market Training and Retraining.* Toronto: Faculty of Law: Centre for the Study of State and Market, University of Toronto.

Betcherman, Gordon, Kathryn McMullen and Katie Davidman. 1998. *Training for the New Economy: A Synthesis Report.* Ottawa: Canadian Policy Research Networks.

Bhyat, Zaheer A. 1995. "The Ontario Training and Adjustment Board (OTAB): A Partnership Response to the Impact of Global Economic Change." Unpublished MA thesis in the Graduate Department of Education, University of Toronto.

Borins, Sandford F. 1983. *The Language of the Skies: The Bilingual Air Traffic Control Conflict in Canada.* Kingston and Montreal: McGill-Queen's University Press and the Institute of Public Administration of Canada.

Bradford, Neil. 1998. "Ontario's Experiment with Sectoral Initiatives: Labour Market and Industrial Policy, 1985-1996," in *Forging Business-Labour Partnerships: The Emergence of Sector Councils in Canada*, ed. Morley Gunderson and Andrew Sharpe. Toronto: University of Toronto Press, pp. 158-92.

Breton, Raymond. 1977. *The Canadian Condition: A Guide to Research in Public Policy.* Montreal: Institute for Research on Public Policy.

Brint, Steven and Jerome Karabel. 1989. *The Diverted Dream: Community Colleges and the Promise of Educational Opportunity in America, 1900-1985.* New York: Oxford University Press.

——. 1991. "Institutional Origins and Transformations: The Case of the American Community Colleges," in *The New Institutionalism in Organizational Analysis*, ed. Walter W. Powell and Paul J. Dimaggio. Chicago: University of Chicago Press, pp. 337-60.

Brown, Paul M. 1997. *Genesis, Termination and Succession in the Life-Cycle of Organizations: The Case of the Maritime Resource Management Service.* Monograph No. 19. Toronto: Institute of Public Administration of Canada.

Bruderl, Josef and Rudolf Schussler. 1990. "Organizational Mortality: The Liability of Newness and Adolescence," *Administrative Science Quarterly*, 35:530-47.

Cameron, Kim *et al.* 1987. "Organizational Effects of Decline and Turbulence," *Administrative Science Quarterly*, 32:222-40.

Campbell, Robert M. 1992. "The Conservatives and the Unemployed," in *How Ottawa Spends 1992-93: The Politics of Competitiveness*, ed. Frances Abele. Ottawa: Carleton University Press, pp. 23-56.

Canada. Employment and Immigration Canada (EIC). 1981. *Labour Market Development in the 1980's*. Report of the Task Force on Labour Market Development. Ottawa: Supply and Services Canada.

——. 1984. *Consultation Paper: Training*. Ottawa: Supply and Services Canada.

——. 1990. *EIC on the Move to Meet the Employment Programming Objectives of the Labour Force Development Strategy*. Ottawa: Employment Policies Branch.

Canada. House of Commons Standing Committee on Human Resources Development. 1995. *Security, Opportunities and Fairness: Canadians Renewing Their Social Programs*. Minutes of Proceeding and Evidence of the Standing Committee, First Session of the Thirty-fifth Parliament. Ottawa: Supply and Services Canada.

Canada. Human Resources Development Canada (HRDC). 1996. "Getting Canadians Back to Work: A Proposal to Provinces and Territories for a New Partnership in the Labour Market," press release, 30 May.

Canadian Labour Force Development Board (CLFDB). 1995. *Annual Report 1994-95*. Ottawa: Canadian Labour Force Development Board.

Chaison, Gary N., Barbara Bigelow and Edward Ottensmeyer. 1993. "Unions and Legitimacy: A Conceptual Refinement," *Research in the Sociology of Organizations*, 12:139-66.

Child, J. 1972. "Organizational Structure, Environment and Performance: The Role of Strategic Choice," *Sociology*, 6 (June):1-22.

Clark, Burton R. 1956. "Organizational Adaptation and Precarious Values: A Case Study," *American Sociological Review*, 21(3):327-36.

——. 1958. *Adult Education in Transition: A Study of Institutional Insecurity*. Berkeley: University of California Press.

——. 1960. *The Open Door College: A Case Study*. New York: McGraw-Hill.

Coleman, Paul. 1976. "Industrial Training in Ontario: From Vision to Reality," *Adult Training* (Canada Manpower and Immigration), 2:24-30.

Coleman, William D. and Henry J. Jacek. 1983. "The Roles and Activities of Business Interest Associations in Canada," *Canadian Journal of Political Science*, 16(2):257-80.

Council of Ontario Universities. 1993. *Brief to the Standing Committee on Resources Development on Bill 96.* Toronto, 15 February.

Crispo, John *et al.* 1972. *Report on the Organizational Placement of the Industrial Training Branch of the Ontario Department of Labour.* Submitted to the Ontario Treasury Board, January.

Crozier, Michael. 1964. *The Bureaucratic Phenomenon.* Chicago: University of Chicago Press.

Cyert, Richard M. and James G. March. 1963. *A Behavioral Theory of the Firm.* Englewood Cliffs, NJ: Prentice-Hall.

Davies, James B. 1986. "Training and Skill Development," in *Adapting to Change: Labour Market Adjustment in Canada,* ed. W. Craig Riddell. Toronto: University of Toronto Press, pp. 163-219.

Dehli, Kari. 1993. "Subject to the New Global Economy: Power and Positioning in Ontario Labour Market Policy Formation," *Studies in Political Economy,* 41 (Summer):83-110.

Dell'Aringa, C. and M.S. Lodovici. 1992. "Industrial Relations and Economic Performance," in *Participation in Policy-Making: The Role of Trade Unions and Employer's Associations,* ed. T. Treu. New York: Walter de Gruyter, pp. 26-58.

deLeon, Peter. 1978. "A Theory of Policy Termination," in *The Policy Cycle,* ed. Judith May and Aaron Wildavsky. Beverley Hills: Sage Publications.

Department of Education. 1967. *Colleges of Applied Arts and Technology: Basic Documents* (Statement in the Legislature: Introducing Colleges of Applied Arts and Technology in Ontario, 21 May 1965). Toronto: Queen's Printer.

DiMaggio, Paul J. and Walter W. Powell. 1991. "Introduction," in *The New Institutionalism in Organizational Analysis,* ed. Walter W. Powell and Paul J. Dimaggio. Chicago: University of Chicago Press, pp. 1-38.

Dobell, A.R. and S.H. Mansbridge. 1986. *The Social Policy Process in Canada.* Montreal: Institute for Research on Public Policy.

Dowling, John and Jeffrey Pfeffer. 1975. "Organizational Legitimacy: Social Values and Organizational Behaviour," *Pacific Sociological Review,* 18(1):122-36.

Downs, Anthony. 1967. *Inside Bureaucracy.* Boston: Little, Brown and Co.

Dryden, Ken. 1986. *Report of the Ontario Youth Commissioner.* Toronto: Queen's Printer for Ontario.

Dupré, Stefan *et al.* 1973. *Federalism and Policy Development: The Case Study of Adult Occupational Training in Ontario.* Toronto: University of Toronto Press.

Dymond, W.R. (Chairman). 1973. *Training for Ontario's Future: Report of the Task Force on Industrial Training*. Toronto: Ministry of Colleges and Universities.

Ebaugh, Helen R.F. 1993. *Women and the Vanishing Cloister: Organizational Decline in Catholic Orders in the United States*. New Brunswick, NJ: Rutgers University Press.

Economic Council of Canada. *Education and Training in Canada*. Ottawa: Supply and Services Canada.

Edney, Debbie. 1993. "The Evolution of Adult Education: Is there a Role for School Boards in OTAB?" *Education Today*, November/December, pp. 14-19.

Ekos Research Associates. 1996. *Developing Skills in the Canadian Workplace: The Results of the Workplace Training Survey*. Prepared for Human Resources Development Canada and the Canadian Policy Research Networks. Ottawa: Ekos Research Associates.

Evan, William M. 1966. "The Organizational Set: Toward a Theory of Interorganizational Relations," in *Approaches to Organizational Design*, ed. James D. Thompson. Pittsburgh: University of Pittsburgh Press, pp. 173-88.

Evans, Brendan. 1992. *The Politics of the Training Market: From Manpower Services Commission to Training and Enterprise Councils*. London: Routledge.

Frantz, Janet E. 1992. "Reviving and Revising a Termination Model," *Policy Sciences*, 25:175-89.

Freeman, John *et al.* 1983. "The Liability of Newness: Age Dependence in Organizational Death Rates," *American Sociological Review*, 48:692-710.

Giles, Anthony. 1989. "Canadian Labour Market Policy and Flexible Employment Systems," in *Flexibility and Labour Markets in Canada and the United States*, ed. G. Laflamme *et al.* Geneva: International Institute for Labour Studies, International Labour Organisation, pp. 237-49.

*The Globe and Mail*. 1992. "Agency to Oversee Job Training in Ontario To Be Set Up over 18 Months," 24 November, p. A5.

Good, David A. 1980. "Notes on Methodology," in *The Politics of Anticipation: Making Canadian Federal Tax Policy*. Ottawa: School of Public Administration, Carleton University, pp. 199-201.

Gouldner, Alvin. 1954. *Patterns of Industrial Bureaucracy*. New York: The Free Press.

Greenhalgh, L. 1983. "Organizational Decline," *Research in the Sociology of Organizations*, 2:231-76.

Guest, Robert H. 1962. *Organizational Change: The Effect of Successful Leadership*. Homewood, Ill: Dorsey Press and Irwin.

Haddow, Rodney. 1995*a*. "Federalism and Training Policy in Canada: Institutional Barriers to Economic Adjustment," in *New Trends in Canadian Federalism*, ed. François Rocher and Miriam Smith. Peterborough, ON: Broadview Press, pp. 338-68.

———. 1995*b*. "Canada's Experiment with Labour Market Neocorporatism," in *Labour Market Polarization and Social Policy Reform*, ed. Keith G. Banting and Charles M. Beach. Kingston: School of Policy Studies, Queen's University, pp. 205-32.

———. 1998. "Reforming Labour-Market Policy Governance: The Quebec Experience," *Canadian Public Administration,* 41(3):343-68.

Haddow, Rodney and Andrew Sharpe. 1997. "Labour Force Development Boards: A Viable Model?" in *Social Partnerships for Training*, ed. Sharpe and Haddow, pp. 291-318.

Hall, Richard H. 1991. *Organizations: Structures, Processes and Outcomes.* Englewood Cliffs, NJ: Prentice Hall.

Hambrick, Donald C. and Richard A. D'Aveni. 1988. "Large Corporate Failures as Downward Spirals," *Administrative Science Quarterly,* 33:1-23.

Hannan, Michael T. and John Freeman. 1977. "The Population of Organizations," *American Journal of Sociology,* 82(4):929-66.

———. 1983. "Niche Width and the Dynamics of Organizational Populations," *American Journal of Sociology,* 88(6):1116-45.

———. 1988. "The Ecology of Organizational Mortality: American Labor Unions, 1836-1985," *American Journal of Sociology,* 94(1):25-52.

Hannigan, John and Rodney Kueneman. 1977. "Legitimacy and Public Organizations: A Case Study," *Canadian Journal of Sociology,* 2(1):125-35.

*Hansard* - Official Report of Proceedings Legislative Assembly of Ontario, Toronto: Queen's Printer for Ontario, excerpts from 1984 to 1990.

Hayak, Friedrich. 1973. *Rules and Order.* Chicago: University of Chicago Press.

Heclo, Hugh *Modern Social Politics in Britain and Sweden.* New Haven: Yale University Press, 1974.

Hedberg, Bo. 1981. "How Organizations Learn and Unlearn," in *Handbook of Organizational Design*, ed. Paul C. Nystrom and William Starbuck. Oxford: Oxford University Press.

Hogwood, Brian W. and B. Guy Peters. 1982. "The Dynamics of Policy Change: Policy Succession," *Policy Sciences,* 14:225-45.

Hout, John. 1989. "Keeping Workers in their Place: The Role of the Community Colleges," in *It's Our Own Knowledge: Labour, Public Education and Skills*

*Training*, ed. Nancy Jackson. Toronto: Our Schools/Our Selves Education Foundation, pp. 31-38.

Howlett, M. and M. Ramesh. 1993. "Patterns of Policy Instrument Choice: Policy Styles, Policy Learning and the Privatization Experience," *Policy Studies Review*, 12 (Spring/Summer):3-24.

Hrebiniak, Lawrence and William Joyce. 1985. "Organizational Adaptation: Strategic Choice and Environmental Determinism," *Administrative Science Quarterly*, 30:336-49.

Hum, Derek and Wayne Simpson. 1996. *Maintaining a Competitive Workforce: Employer-Based Training in the Canadian Economy*. Montreal: The Institute for Research on Public Policy.

Jackson, Nancy, ed. 1992. *Training for What? Labour Perspectives on Job Training*. Toronto: Our Schools/Our Selves Education Foundation.

Katzenbach, E.L. 1958. "The Horse Cavalry in the 20th Century – A Study in Policy Response," *Public Policy*, 8:120-49.

Kaufman, Herbert. 1976. *Are Government Organizations Immortal?* Washington, DC: The Brookings Institution.

Klassen, Thomas R. 1995. "The Process of Organizational Decline and Death: Internal and External Factors Precipitating the Decline of the Ontario Ministry of Skills Development 1985-1993." Unpublished PhD dissertation. Toronto: Department of Sociology, University of Toronto.

———. 1996. "Organizational Design and Precarious Values: The Rise and Fall of Ontario's Ministry of Skills Development," *Canadian Public Administration*, 39(2):117-35.

———. 1999a. "The Federal-Provincial Labour Market Development Agreements: Brave New Model of Cooperation?" Paper prepared for the Institute of Intergovernmental Relations, Queen's University, Kingston, Ontario.

———. 1999b. "Job Market Training: The Social Union in Practice," *Policy Options*, 20(10):40-44.

Klassen, Thomas R. and Daniel Buchanan. 1997. "Getting It Backward: Economy and Welfare in Ontario 1985-1995," *Canadian Public Policy/Analyse de politiques*, 23(3):333-38.

Klassen, Thomas R. and Suzanne LeBlanc. 1993a. "Methodological Issues in Sociological Research on Public Policy: Utilizing Government Documents," *Society*, 17(1):9-13.

———. 1993b. "Methodological Issues in Sociological Research on Public Policy: Utilizing Interviews," *Society*, 17(2):21-26.

Kroeger, Arthur. 1995. "Comments," on "Canada's Experiment with Labour Market Neocorporatism," by Rodney Haddow, in *Labour Market Polarization and Social Policy Reform*, ed. Keith G. Banting and Charles M. Beach. Kingston: School of Policy Studies, Queen's University, pp. 233-35.

Landau, Martin. 1969. "Redundancy, Rationality, and the Problem of Duplication and Overlap," *Public Administration Review*, 29(4):346-58.

———. 1973. "On the Concept Of a Self-Correcting Organization," *Public Administration Review* (November/December):533-42.

Lerner, Allan W. 1986. "There is More than One Way To Be Redundant," *Administration & Society*, 18(3):334-59.

Lester, Richard A. 1996. *Manpower Planning in a Free Society*. Princeton, NJ: Princeton University Press.

Levine, Sol and Paul E. White. 1961. "Exchange as a Conceptual Framework for the Study of Interorganizational Relationships," *Administrative Science Quarterly*, 5 (March):583-601.

Levitt, Barbara and James G. March. 1988. "Organizational Learning," *Annual Review of Sociology*, 14:314-40.

Liberal Party Task Force on Jobs for Youth (John Sweeney, chairman). 1982/83. *Report*. Toronto: Liberal Party.

Lindblom, Charles E. 1958. "The Science of 'Muddling-Through'," *Public Administration Review*, 19 (Spring):79-89.

Lindquist, Evert A. 1992. "Public Managers and Policy Communities: Learning to Meet New Challenges," *Canadian Public Administration*, 35(2):127-59.

Lindquist, Evert A. and Graham White. 1994. "Streams, Springs, and Stones: Ontario Public Service Reform in the 1980s and the 1990s," *Canadian Public Administration*, 37(2):267-301.

Lowe, Graham and Harvey Krahn. 1988. *Working, Industry and Canadian Society*. Scarborough: Nelson Canada.

Mahon, Rianne. 1990. "Adjusting to Win? The New Tory Training Initiative," in *How Ottawa Spends 1990-91: Tracking the Second Agenda*, ed. Katherine Graham. Ottawa: Carleton University Press, pp. 73-111.

Management Board of Cabinet. 1982. *Policy Development*. Ontario Public Service Management Series No. 21-2. Toronto: Queen's Printer for Ontario.

———. 1983a. *The Cabinet and Central Agencies: Roles and Responsibilities*. Ontario Public Service Management Series No. 8-1. Toronto: Queen's Printer for Ontario.

———. 1983b. *Reorganizing*. Ontario Public Service Management Series. Toronto: Queen's Printer for Ontario.

——. 1986-87. *Expenditures Estimates*, Vol. 3, *Economic Policy*. Toronto: Queen's Printer for Ontario.

——. 1990/91. *Expenditures Estimates*, Vol. 2. Toronto: Queen's Printer for Ontario.

March, James G. 1988. *Decisions and Organizations*. Oxford: Basil Blackwell.

Martin, D'Arcy. 1992. "Unions and Training in Ontario," in *Training for What?* ed. Nacy Jackson, pp. 66-75.

——. 1995. *Thinking Union: Activism and Education in Canada's Labour Movement*. Toronto: Between the Lines.

McBride, Stephen. 1992. *Not Working: State, Unemployment, and Neo-Conservatism in Canada*. Toronto: University of Toronto Press.

——. 1994. "The Political Economy of Ontario's Labour Market Policy," in *Continuities and Discontinuities: The Political Economy of Social Welfare and Labour Market Policy in Canada*, ed. Andrew Johnson, Stephen McBride and Patrick Smith. Toronto: University of Toronto Press, pp. 268-90.

——. 1996. "The Continuing Crisis of Social Democracy: Ontario Social Contract in Perspective," *Studies in Political Economy*, 50 (Summer):65-93.

McFadyen, Craig. 1994. "State, Society and the Development of Active Labour Market Policy in Canada: The Case of the Canadian Jobs Strategy." Unpublished PhD dissertation, Department of Political Science, University of Toronto.

Meltz, Noah. 1990. "The Evolution of Worker Training: The Canadian Experience," in *New Developments in Worker Training: A Legacy for the 1990's*, ed. Louis A. Ferman *et al.* Madison, WI: Industrial Relations Research Association Series.

Merton, Robert K. 1972. "Insiders and Outsiders: A Chapter in the Sociology of Knowledge," *American Journal of Sociology*, 78(1):9-47.

Meyer, Marshall W. 1979. *Change in Public Bureaucracies*. Cambridge: Cambridge University Press.

Meyer, Marshall W. and Lynne G. Zucker. 1989. *Permanently Failing Organizations*. Newbury Park, CA: Sage Publications.

Miller, Frank. 1985. *Enterprise Ontario: Opportunities for People*. Toronto, 22 March.

Miller, Riel. 1993. "Education and Training in the Knowledge Economy: Prospects and Missed Opportunities," in *How Ottawa Spends 1994-95: Making Change*, ed. Susan D. Phillips. Ottawa: Carleton University Press, pp. 339-71.

Minister of Finance. 1995. *Jumpstart Program Aims to Boost Youth Employment*. Press Release, 27 April. Toronto.

Ministry of Government Services. Various Years. *Government of Ontario Telephone Directory* (published twice yearly). Toronto: Queen's Printer for Ontario.

Ministry of Skills Development (MSD). 1985. *A Bill to Establish the New Ministry of Skills Development*. News Release. Toronto. 11 June.

———. 1986*a*. *Report of the Training Services Task Force*. Internal Document.

———. 1986*b*. *Breaking New Ground*. Toronto: Queen's Printer for Ontario.

———. 1987*a*. *Out of School Youth in Ontario: Their Labour Market Experience*. Toronto: Queen's Printer for Ontario.

———. 1987*b*. *Literacy the Basics of Growth*. Toronto: Queen's Printer for Ontario.

———. 1988*a*. *Programs & Services*. Toronto: Queen's Printer for Ontario.

———. 1988*b*. *Skills Programs*. Toronto: Queen's Printer for Ontario.

———. 1989*a*. *Literacy and Basic Skills*.

———. 1989*b*. *Literacy: The Basics of Growth*.

———. 1989*c*. *Occupational Literacy: A Training Profile Development Project*. Toronto: Queen's Printer for Ontario.

———. 1989*d*. *Strategic Directions*. Toronto: Queen's Printer for Ontario.

———. 1989/90. *Estimates Background Material*. Toronto: Queen's Printer for Ontario.

Ministry of Treasury and Economics. 1986. *Ontario Statistics*. Toronto: Queen's Printer for Ontario.

———. 1979/80-1995/96. *Public Accounts of Ontario*, Vol. 1. *Financial Statements*. Toronto: Queen's Printer for Ontario.

Molnar, Joseph J. and David B. Rogers. 1979. "A Comparative Model of Interorganizational Conflict," *Administrative Science Quarterly*, 24 (September):405-25.

Nachmias, David. 1982. "Organizational Conflict in Public Bureaus: A Model," *Administration & Society*, 14(3):283-98.

Newman, Michael. 1993. *The Third Contract: Theory and Practice in Trade Union Training*. Sydney: Stewart Victor Publishing.

Nystrom, P.C. and W.H. Starbuck. 1984. "To Avoid Organizational Crisis, Unlearn," *Organizational Dynamics* (Spring):53-65.

O'Connor, James. 1973. *The Fiscal Crisis of the State*. New York: St. Martin's Press.

Office of the Provincial Auditor of Ontario. 1995. *Ontario Training and Adjustment Board Financial Statements for the Year Ended March 31, 1995*. Toronto: Office of the Provincial Auditor of Ontario.

Ontario. 1985. *Bill 9, An Act to Establish the Ministry of Skills Development*, The Honourable P. Gillies, Minister of Skills Development, First Reading, Toronto, 11 June.

———. Cabinet Office. 1987. *Cabinet Submission Guidelines*. Toronto: Queen's Park, 31 March.

Ontario Federation of Labour. 1997. *Labour's Voice in Ontario*. Publication produced for the 1997 convention. Toronto: Ontario Federation of Labour.

Ontario Liberal Party. 1995. *Ontario Liberal Plan*. Toronto: Ontario Liberal Party.

Ontario Manpower Commission. 1984. *Training in Industry: A Survey of Employer-Sponsored Programs in Ontario*. Toronto: Ontario Manpower Commission.

Ontario Training and Adjustment Board (OTAB). 1991. *Skills to Meet the Challenge: A Training Partnership for Growth*. Toronto: OTAB secretariat.

———. 1992a. *OTAB Update*, No. 1. Toronto: OTAB.

———. 1992b. *Fact Sheet* ("What is OTAB?"). Toronto: OTAB, 23 November.

———. 1994a. *Co-Chairs' Report*. Toronto: OTAB, May.

———. 1994b. *Annual Report 1994*. Toronto: Queen's Printer for Ontario.

———. 1995a. *Annual Report 1995*. Toronto: Queen's Printer for Ontario.

———. 1995b. *Corporate Annual Plan*. Toronto: Queen's Printer for Ontario.

———. Policy Staff. 1995. *Potential Impact of the 1995 Ontario Progressive Platform*, 1 June. Toronto: OTAB.

Organisation for Economic Cooperation and Development (OECD). 1984. *Employment Outlook 1984*. Paris: OECD.

———. 1993. *Employment Outlook 1993*. Paris: OECD.

———. 1999. *OECD in Figures: 1999 Edition*, Supplement to *OECD Observer*, No. 217/218. Paris: OECD.

Osbaldeston, Gordon. 1992. *Organizing to Govern*, Vol. 1. Toronto: McGraw-Hill Ryerson.

Patrick, Glenda M. 1983. "The Establishment and Development of Colleges of Applied Arts and Technology: A Study of Vocational and Technical Education Policy in the Province of Ontario, 1889 to 1979," PhD Thesis. Toronto: University of Toronto.

Perrow, Charles. 1961. "Organizational Prestige: Some Functions and Dysfunctions," *American Journal of Sociology*, 66(4):335-41.

Pitman, Walter. 1986. *The Report of the Advisor to the Minister of Colleges and Universities on the Governance of the Colleges of Applied Arts and Technology*. Toronto.

Premier's Council. 1989. *Premier Appoints New Members to Premier's Council.* Press Release. Toronto.

——. 1990. *People and Skills in the New Global Economy.* Toronto: Queen's Printer.

Premier's Office. 1985. *Cabinet Appointments.* Press Release, 26 June. Toronto.

——. 1989*a. New Cabinet Appointed.* Press Release, 2 August. Toronto.

——. 1989*b. Press Release,* 6 September. Toronto.

Prince, Michael J. and James J. Rice. 1989. "The Canadian Jobs Strategy: Supply Side Social Policy," in *How Ottawa Spends 1989-90: The Buck Stops Where?* ed. Katherine A. Graham. Ottawa: Carleton University Press, pp. 247-87.

Riddell, Craig W. 1986. "Labour-Management Cooperation in Canada: An Overview," in *Labour-Management in Canada,* ed. W. Graig Riddell. Toronto: University of Toronto Press, pp. 1-56.

Ritti, Richard R. and Jonathan H. Silver. 1986. "Early Processes of Institutionalization: The Dramaturgy of Exchange in Interorganizational Relations," *Administrative Science Quarterly,* 31:25-42.

Rogers, David L. and David A. Whetten. 1982. *Interorganizational Coordination: Theory, Research, and Implementation.* Ames, IA: Iowa State University Press.

Schmid, G. 1994. *Labor Market Institutions in Europe: A Socioeconomic Evaluation of Performance.* Armonkk, NY: M.E. Sharpe.

Schmid, G. and K. Schomann. 1994. "Institutional Choice and Flexible Coordination: A Socioeconomic Evaluation of Labor Market Policy in Europe," in *Labor Market Institutions in Europe,* ed. Schmid, pp. 9-58.

Schmitter, Phillipe. 1974. "Still the Century of Corporatism?" in *The New Corporatism: Social-Political Structures in the Iberian World,* ed. Frederick B. Pike and Thomas Stritch. Notre Dame: University of Notre Dame Press, pp. 85-131.

Scott, Richard W. 1991. "Unpacking Institutional Arguments," in *The New Institutionalism in Organizational Analysis,* ed. Walter W. Powell and Paul J. DiMaggio. Chicago: University of Chicago Press, pp. 164-82.

——. 1992. *Organizations: Rational, Natural and Open Systems,* 3d ed. Englewood Cliffs, NJ: Prentice-Hall.

——. 1995. *Institutions and Organizations.* Thousand Oaks, CA: Sage Publications.

Scotton, Geoffrey. 1992. "'Pioneer' Agencies Circle the Wagons," *Financial Post,* 7 November, p. 11.

Selznick, Philip. 1948. "Foundations of a Theory of Organizations," *American Sociological Review,* 13:25-35.

——. 1949. *TVA and the Grass Roots: A Study in the Sociology of Formal Organization.* Berkeley: University of California Press.

——. 1957. *Leadership in Administration: A Sociological Interpretation.* New York: Harper & Row.

Shapiro, Bernard J. 1989. *Skills Development: A New Direction.* Report to the Secretary of Cabinet. Toronto.

Sharpe, Andrew and Rodney Haddow, eds. 1997. *Social Partnerships for Training: Canada's Experiment with Labour Force Development Boards.* Kingston: Caledon Institute of Social Policy and School of Policy Studies, Queen's University.

Shields, John and B. Mitchell Evans 1998. *Shrinking the State: Globalization and Public Administration "Reform."* Halifax: Fernwood Publishing.

Simeon, Richard. 1976. "Studying Public Policy," *Canadian Journal of Political Science,* 9:548-80.

Simon, Herbert A., Donald W. Smithburg and Victor A. Thompson. 1965. "The Struggle for Organizatioal Survival," in *Bureaucratic Power in National Politics,* ed. Francis E. Rourke. Boston: Little, Brown and Co.

Smith, D.H. and J. Dixon. 1973. "The Voluntary Society," in *Challenge to Leadership: Managing in a Changing World.* New York: The Conference Board, pp. 202-27.

Speirs, Rosemary. 1985. "Liberals May Abandon Idea of Skills Development Ministry," *The Toronto Star,* 15 July.

——. 1986. *Out of the Blue: The Fall of the Tory Dynasty in Ontario.* Toronto: Macmillan.

*The Toronto Star.* 1988. "Liberals Reneged on Job Training Rae Charges," 20 May.

Statistics Canada. 1990. *The Labour Force,* Cat. No. 71-001 (monthly). Ottawa: Supply and Services Canada.

——. 1996. *Historical Labour Force Statistics – 1995,* Cat. No. 71-201. Ottawa: Statistics Canada.

Stewart, Edward E. 1989. *Cabinet Government in Ontario: A View from Inside.* Halifax: Institute for Research on Public Policy.

Stinchcombe, Arthur L. 1965. "Social Structure and Organizations," in *Handbook of Organizations,* ed. James G. March. Chicago: Rand-McNally, pp. 142-70.

Thung, Mady A. 1976. *The Precarious Organization: Sociological Explorations of the Church's Mission and Structure.* The Hague: Mouton & Co.

Thurow, Lester. 1993. "Six Revolutions, Six Economic Challenges," *Toronto Star* 28 January, p. A21.

Treu, Tiziano. 1992. "Tripartite Social Policy-Making: An Overview," in *Participation in Public Policy-Making: The Role of Trade Unions and Employers' Associations*, ed. Tiziano Treu. Berlin: Walter de Gruyter, pp.1-25.

Tully, Blair. 1986. *Memorandum re: Reorganization of the Ministry of Skills Development.* 9 April.

Tyack, David and Elisabeth Hansot. 1982. *Managers of Virtue: Public School Leadership in America, 1820-1980.* New York: Basic Books.

Veugelers, J.W.P. and Thomas R. Klassen. 1994. "Continuity and Change in Canada's Unemployment-Immigration Linkage," *Canadian Journal of Sociology,* 19(3):351-69.

Walizer, Michael H. and Paul L. Wienir. 1978. *Research Methods and Analysis: Searching for Relationships.* New York: Harper & Row.

Walmsley, Gary L. and Mayer N. Zald. 1973. *The Political Economy of Public Organizations.* Lexington, MA: Lexington Books.

Wever, Kirsten S. 1995. *Negotiating Competitiveness: Employment Relations and Organizational Innovation in Germany and the United States.* Boston: Harvard Business School Press.

Whetten, David A. 1981. "Sources, Responses and Effects of Organizational Decline," in *The Organizational Life Cycle: Issues in the Creation, Transformation and Decline of Organizations*, ed. John R. Kimberley and Robert H. Miles. San Francisco: Jossey-Bass, Inc., pp. 342-76.

——. 1987. "Organizational Growth and Decline Processes," *Annual Review of Sociology,* 13:335-58.

White, Graham. 1989. *The Ontario Legislature: A Political Analysis.* Toronto: University of Toronto Press.

——. 1993. "Traffic Pile Ups at Queen's Park: Recent Ontario Transitions," in *Taking Power: Managing Government Transitions*, ed. Donald J. Savoie. Toronto: Institute of Public Administration of Canada, pp. 115-43.

Wholey, Douglas *et al.* 1992. "Organizational Size and Failure among Health Maintenance Organizations," *American Sociological Review,* 57 (December):829-42.

Wiewel, Wim and Albert Hunter. 1985. "The Interorganizational Network as a Resource: A Comparative Study on Organizational Genesis," *Administrative Science Quarterly,* 30:482-96.

Wildavsky, A. 1979. *Speaking Truth to Power: The Art and Craft of Policy Analysis.* Toronto: Little, Brown.

Wilson, Benson A. 1984. *Memorandum re: Role and Responsibility of the Ontario Manpower Commission.* 13 April.

Wilson, David N. 1993*a.* "The Effectiveness of Training Boards in Canada," Discussion Paper No. 109. Geneva: Training Policies Branch, International Labour Office.

———. 1993*b.* "The Effectiveness of National Training Boards," Discussion Paper No. 110. Geneva: Training Policies Branch, International Labour Office.

Wolfe, David A. 1997. "Institutional Limits to Labour Market Reform in Ontario: The Short Life and Rapid Demise of the Ontario Training and Adjustment Board," in *Social Partnerships for Training*, ed. Sharpe and Haddow, pp. 155-88.

Wolfe, David A. and Armine Yalnizyan. 1989. *Target on Training: Meeting Worker's Needs in a Changing Economy.* Toronto: Social Planning Council of Metropolitan Toronto.

Young, Greg and Roger Briers. 1996. "The End of OTAB," *Training and Development Guide*, 9 (Summer):4-6.

Zald, Mayer N. 1990. "History, Sociology and Theories," in *Institutions in American Society: Essays in Market, Political and Social Organizations*, ed. John E. Jackson. Ann Arbor: University of Michigan Press.

Zald, Mayer N. and Patricia Denton. 1963. "From Evangelism to General Service: The Transformation of the YMCA," *Administrative Science Quarterly*, 8(2):214-34.

# Index

# Queen's Policy Studies
## Recent Publications

The Queen's Policy Studies Series is dedicated to the exploration of major policy issues that confront governments in Canada and other western nations. McGill-Queen's University Press is the exclusive world representative and distributor of books in the series.

### School of Policy Studies

*The Nonprofit Sector in Canada: Roles and Relationships,* Keith G. Banting (ed.), 2000
Paper ISBN 0-88911-813-2  Cloth ISBN 0-88911-815-9

*Security, Strategy and the Global Economics of Defence Production,* David G. Haglund and S. Neil MacFarlane (eds.), 1999   Paper ISBN 0-88911-875-2  Cloth ISBN 0-88911-877-9

*The Communications Revolution at Work: The Social, Economic and Political Impacts of Technological Change,* Robert Boyce (ed.), 1999   Paper ISBN 0-88911-805-1  Cloth ISBN 0-88911-807-8

*Diplomatic Missions: The Ambassador in Canadian Foreign Policy,* Robert Wolfe (ed.), 1998
Paper ISBN 0-88911-801-9  Cloth ISBN 0-88911-803-5

*Issues in Defence Management,* Douglas L. Bland (ed.), 1998
Paper ISBN 0-88911-809-4  Cloth ISBN 0-88911-811-6

*Canada's National Defence,* vol. 2, *Defence Organization,* Douglas L. Bland (ed.), 1998
Paper ISBN 0-88911-797-7  Cloth ISBN 0-88911-799-3

*Canada's National Defence,* vol. 1, *Defence Policy,* Douglas L. Bland (ed.), 1997
Paper ISBN 0-88911-792-6  Cloth ISBN 0-88911-790-X

### Institute of Intergovernmental Relations

*Managing the Environmental Union: Intergovernmental Relations and Environmental Policy in Canada,* Patrick C. Fafard and Kathryn Harrison (eds.), 2000   ISBN 0-88911-837-X

*Comparing Federal Systems,* 2d ed., Ronald L. Watts, 1999   ISBN 0-88911-835-3

*Canada: The State of the Federation 1999/2000,* vol. 14, *Rebalancing and Decentralizing Fiscal Federalism,* Harvey Lazar (ed.), 2000   Paper ISBN 0-88911-843-4  Cloth ISBN 0-88911-839-6

*Canada: The State of the Federation 1998/99,* vol. 13, *How Canadians Connect,* Harvey Lazar and Tom McIntosh (eds.), 1999   Paper ISBN 0-88911-781-0  Cloth ISBN 0-88911-779-9

*Canada: The State of the Federation 1997,* vol. 12, *Non-Constitutional Renewal,* Harvey Lazar (ed.), 1998
Paper ISBN 0-88911-765-9  Cloth ISBN 0-88911-767-5

### John Deutsch Institute for the Study of Economic Policy

*Room to Manoeuvre? Globalization and Policy Convergence,* Thomas J. Courchene (ed.),
Bell Canada Papers no. 6, 1999   Paper ISBN 0-88911-812-4  Cloth ISBN 0-88911-812-4

*Women and Work,* Richard P. Chaykowski and Lisa M. Powell (eds.), 1999
Paper ISBN 0-88911-808-6  Cloth ISBN 0-88911-806-X

*Equalization: Its Contribution to Canada's Economic and Fiscal Progress,* Robin W. Boadway and Paul A.R. Hobson (eds.), Policy Forum Series no. 36, 1998
Paper ISBN 0-88911-780-2  Cloth IBSN 0-88911-804-3

*Fiscal Targets and Economic Growth,* Thomas J. Courchene and Thomas A. Wilson (eds.),
Roundtable Series no. 12, 1998   Paper ISBN 0-88911-778-0  Cloth ISBN 0-88911-776-4

*The 1997 Federal Budget: Retrospect and Prospect,* Thomas J. Courchene and Thomas A. Wilson (eds.),
Policy Forum Series no. 35, 1997   Paper ISBN 0-88911-774-8  Cloth ISBN 0-88911-772-1

**Available from:**
McGill-Queen's University Press
Tel:   1-800-387-0141 (ON and QC excluding Northwestern ON)
        1-800-387-0172 (all other provinces and Northwestern ON)

E-mail: customer.service@ccmailgw.genpub.com

# The Institute of Public Administration of Canada
# L'Institut d'administration publique du Canada

## The IPAC Monograph Series

*From Bureaucracy to Public Management: The Administrative Culture of the Government of Canada* (July 1999). O.P. Dwivedi and James Iain Gow. ISBN 1-55111-271-X. $26.95/$21.56 (members)

*Citizen Engagement: Lessons in Participation from Local Government* (June 1998) Monograph No. 22. K.A. Graham and S.D. Phillips (eds.). ISBN 0-920715-78-8. 245 pages. $29.95/$24.95 (members)

*Value for Many: The Institute of Public Administration of Canada, 1947-1997* (1997) Monograph No. 21. V. Seymour Wilson. ISBN 0-920715-55-9. 157 pages. $29.95/$24.95 (members)

*The Responsible Public Servant* (1990). Kenneth Kernaghan and John W. Langford. ISBN 0-88645-099-3. 220 pages. $19.95/$15.95 (members)

*New Public Management and Public Administration in Canada* (September 1997). Mohamed Charih and Arthur Daniels (eds.). ISBN 0-920715-54-0. 330 pages. $29.95/$24.95 (members)

*Alternative Service Delivery Sharing Governance in Canada* (1997). Robin Ford and David Zussman (eds.). (second printing) ISBN 0-920715-40-0 (no charge)

*Genesis, Termination and Succession in the Life-Cycle of Organizations: The Case of the Maritime Resource Management Service* (1997) Monograph No. 19. M. Paul Brown. ISBN 0-920715-39-7. 82 pages. $18.00/$14.40 (members)

*So-Called Experts: How American Consultants Remade the Canadian Civil Service 1918-21* (1996) Monograph No. 18. Alasdair Roberts. ISBN 0-920715-38-9. 106 pages. $18.00/$14.40 (members)

*Hard Choices or No Choices: Assessing Program Review* (1995) Monograph No. 17. Amelita Armit and Jacques Bourgault. ISBN 0-920715-37-0. 191 pages. $22.00/$17.00 (members)

*Learning from Others: Administrative Innovations Among Canadian Governments* (1994) Monograph No. 16. James Iain Gow. ISBN 0-920715-22-2. 218 pages. $24.95/$19.95 (members)

*Public Management in a Borderless Economy* (1994) International Seminar. Rodney Dobell and Philip Steenkamp (eds.). ISBN 0-90715-20-6. 140 pages. $19.95/$15.95 (members)

*Decentralization and Power Sharing: Impact on Public Sector Management* (1994) 24th National Seminar. David M. Cameron (ed.). ISBN 0-920715-34-6. 112 pages. $19.95/$15.95 (members).

*Agencies, Boards and Commissions in Canadian Local Government* (1993) Monograph No. 15. Dale Richmond and David Siegel. ISBN 0-920715-19-2. 138 pages. $17.95/$15.95 (members)

*Taking Power: Managing Government Transitions* (1993) Monograph No. 14. Donald J. Savoie. ISBN 0-920715-17-6. 251 pages. $29.95/$23.95 (members)

*City Management in Canada: The Role of the CAO* (1992) Monograph No. 13. T.J. Plunkett. ISBN 0-920715-10-9. 76 pages. $18.14/$16.95 (members)

*Getting the Pink Slip: Severances and Firings in the Senior Public Service* (1990) Monograph No. 12. William A.W. Neilson (ed.). ISBN 0-920715-07-9. 185 pages.$19.95/$15.95 (members)

*Think Globally: Proceedings of the IPAC 42nd Annual Conference* (1990) $25.00 (cloth)

*Do Unto Others: A Conference on Ethics in Government and Business* (11-12 June 1991) ISBN 0-920715-09-5. 202 pages. $19.95/$15.00 (paper)

*Innovations and Trends in Management Development* (1990) 22nd National Seminar. Donald J. Savoie (ed.). ISBN 0-920715-06-0. 117 pages. $19.95/$15.95 (members)

*The Well Performing Government Organization* (1990). James C. McDavid and D. Brian Marson (eds.). ISBN 0-920715-11-7. 178 pages. $22.00/$17.00 (members)

**These publications are available from:**
The Institute of Public Administration of Canada /
L'Institut d'administration publique du Canada
1075 Bay Street, Suite 401, Toronto, Ontario M5S 2B1
Tel: (416) 924-8787 / Fax: (416) 924-4992
E-mail: ntl@ipaciapc.ca
Internet: www.ipaciapc.ca